Questions Answers

Questions & Answers

J. Vernon McGee

THOMAS NELSON PUBLISHERS • NASHVILLE

Published in Nashville, Tennessee, by Thomas Nelson, Inc., and distributed in Canada by Lawson Falle, Ltd., Cambridge, Ontario.

Printed in the United States of America.

Unless otherwise noted Scripture quotations are from the KING JAMES VERSION OF THE BIBLE. Copyright © 1976, by Thomas Nelson Publishers, Inc.

Scripture quotations noted ASV are from the American Standard Version.

Scripture quotations noted NKJV are from THE NEW KING JAMES VERSION of the Bible. Copyright © 1979, 1980, 1982, Thomas Nelson Publishers, Inc.

ISBN 0-8407-7580-6

Printed in the United States of America

1 2 3 4 5 6 7 — 95 94 93 92 91 90

CONTENTS

close to me? Will God take me back again? I want to feel secure.

What does a person have to do to have contentment in the heart? Or maybe a better way to say it is, how can I have peace of mind and completely get rid of that ever-lingering feeling of insecurity?

GIVING   35

I'm a new Christian and I really want to support my church with my tithe. But my husband says we don't have to donate anything, because tithing is Old Testament and Christians aren't under the Law anymore. What do you think?

How should you give money you've set aside as a faith promise? In our church, some feel your faith promise is between you and the Lord and can be sent directly to missionaries, for example. Others insist that a gift must first be given to the church but can be designated by the giver as to where it should be sent.

NATURE OF MAN   38

I have understood you to say that we all have the carnal nature, or the "old man" of sin, but that we cannot get rid of it. If that is so, how do you interpret Romans 7:19–25; 8:1–2?

PRIESTHOOD OF BELIEVERS   40

What do you mean when you say, "I am a catholic priest but not a Roman Catholic"?

RELATIONSHIPS   41

I am against divorce, but I heard a minister say that divorce is all right as long as God didn't join you together in the first place. My Sunday school teacher says every situation is different, and God expects us to use common sense. Would you please comment on both of these views?

I was divorced by my alcoholic, unfaithful husband many years ago. Now a wonderful Christian man has entered my life. Is it all right to marry again?

My fiancé says that we should start sleeping together before we get married so we will have an established relationship when we get married. He says it isn't wrong because we're engaged. What does the Bible say?

SIN AND FORGIVENESS 47

In John 20:23 Jesus said, "Whosoever sins ye remit, they are remitted unto them; and whosoever sins ye retain, they are retained." How can we do this?

Would you please differentiate between faults and sins? You have said we should confess our *faults* to one another but our *sins* to God. So many faults and sins overlap one another. Is there a line that can be drawn?

Is there Scripture to prove that a living body in the Spirit can live without sin?

SUICIDE 50

I was completely surprised when one of my friends from church committed suicide. How could a Christian kill himself?

TEMPTATION 51

Does God tempt man? I have always believed James 1:13 and have quoted it to myself. But Luke 11:4 hit me like a rock one day. Would you explain "lead me not into temptation"?

SECTION TWO: THE LIFE OF CHRIST

sat. I know nothing about horses, mules, or donkeys, but since He rode on an unbroken donkey,
wouldn't that make this a miracle?

LAST SUPPER   67

What is the significance of communion? Is it really
the body and blood of Jesus?

You seem to bypass John 13:14 in your preaching,
so I wonder what you think about foot washing.
What was the significance of Christ's washing the
disciples' feet?

GARDEN OF GETHSEMANE   72

In Luke 22:44 we are told that in the Garden of
Gethsemane the Lord's "sweat was as it were great
drops of blood." Was He actually sweating blood? I
have heard some say His sweat was *like* big drops
of blood, but not blood.

Some believe Jesus was praying to see if there were
some other way instead of going to the cross. But
since this had been planned by Jesus and the Father,
and He came to bear our sins that we might be
saved, then it would seem He would know there
was no other way for us to be saved except by the
cross. So why would He try to find another way?

What did Jesus mean when He asked in the Garden
of Gethsemane, "Let this cup pass from me"? I
have always believed Jesus' prayer in the Garden
was not to avoid bearing our sins and dying for us,
but to protect Him from Satan, who was there in the
Garden about to take His life before He got to the
cross. Hebrews 5:7 says, "Who in the days of his
flesh, when he had offered up prayers and supplications with strong crying and tears unto him that
was able to save him from death, and was heard in
that he feared." Isn't that telling us God did hear
and saved Him from dying in the Garden?

Regarding Matthew 26:39, did Jesus know when He
prayed, "O my Father, if it be possible, let this cup

pass from me: nevertheless not as I will, but as thou wilt," that He would be forsaken?

TRIAL

Is it true that the Jews are responsible for Christ's death?

What was the Roman responsibility for Christ's death?

CRUCIFIXION

Did Jesus remain on the cross overnight?

When Christ was crucified, why did He say, "My God, my God," instead of "My Father, my Father, why hast thou forsaken me" (Matt. 27:46)?

You declared that Christ's cross was probably one upright piece of wood. How in the world could anyone make a cross from one upright chunk of a tree?

If Jesus had brothers and sisters, why did our Lord request on the cross that the apostle John take care of His mother Mary? Why couldn't the brothers and sisters take care of her?

DEATH

Recently I heard that when Jesus went to hell to set captives free, He suffered the torments of hell to complete our redemption. Do you know a Scripture that would support or refute this teaching?

RESURRECTION

Someone who came to my door said that Jesus didn't resurrect bodily but only as a spirit. What does the Bible say?

I would like to know where in the Bible it says that Christ arose on Easter Sunday. I have found only the following:

- Matthew 28:1: "In the end of the sabbath, as it began to dawn toward the first day of the week . . ."

- Mark 16:1: "And when the sabbath was passed . . ."
- Luke 24:1–2: "Now upon the first day of the week, very early in the morning . . . they found the stone rolled away from the sepulchre."
- John 20:1: "The first day of the week . . . when it was yet dark . . ."

Why did Christ tell Mary not to touch Him before He ascended?

When was Jesus glorified? When Judas left the Upper Room, Jesus said He was now glorified. I've always been taught that Jesus was not glorified until after He went to heaven, but John 13:31 seems to refute that. Please explain.

Is Christ with us now or is He coming at some future time?

I have assumed that when Jesus said He was going away temporarily He was referring to the Resurrection. And His return will be the Second Coming. What do you think?

SECTION THREE: DOCTRINE

Why did God create angels? What is their function? Do we have guardian angels?

Must I be baptized to be saved? Why do some churches consider baptism by immersion to be so important?

You say water baptism is not necessary for our salvation. How do you explain 1 Peter 3:21?

Where does it say, "One faith, one Lord, one baptism"? I understand this verse to refer to one's being born again and joined to the body of Christ, not to water baptism.

BIBLE 96

Is every word of the Bible true?

Our pastor preaches strong gospel on Sunday. But in his Bible study he tells us that the story of creation is not the story of the creation of the world but rather a story of the creation of the Jewish race; that there were people living in China long before the time Adam and Eve were brought into existence; that Moses never wrote the first five books of the Bible and that there was no writing before the time of Ezra; that following the Revolutionary War all the Christians that were left in the United States were Methodists; and that the World Council of Churches will bring about the return of the Lord.

What does it mean to say the Bible has been *inspired*?

Why does the Roman Catholic Bible have more books than the Protestant Bible?

BOOK OF LIFE 100

Can one's name be blotted out from the book of life, as Revelation 3:5 seems to suggest?

CREATION 108

My pastor says the Genesis account of creation was never meant to be taken literally and that any thinking person knows that evolution is true. What do you think?

How long did it take God to create everything? Was it really in just six 24-hour days?

Did dinosaurs really exist? Why didn't Noah take them on the ark?

that it takes place at the end of Revelation 3. I recently came across something that makes me wonder about this timing. First Corinthians 15:51–52, which I believe refers to the Rapture, says that these things shall occur "at the last trump." Could this refer to the seventh trumpet in Revelation 10:7? And, considering Revelation 11:15 and the end of the chapter, could the statement about the mystery of God being finished refer to the church age?

Does Matthew 24, especially verses 29–31, refer to the Rapture?

Please explain the seven trumpets mentioned in Revelation. Which one is the "last trump"?

GOD   125

If God is all-good and all-powerful, why is there so much evil and suffering in the world today?

What is God like?

Someone from another church told me that the word *trinity* is not in the Bible and was made up by the early church. Now I am confused. Is the doctrine of the Trinity true? Where is it in the Bible?

GUIDANCE   132

Does God have a will for my life, and how can I tell what He wants me to do?

HEAVEN   135

Will we know our loved ones in heaven? Do you think we may be able to visit with each other there?

I believe that when Jesus ascended He took the Old Testament saints from paradise with Him to heaven. But Acts 2:34 says that David has not ascended into heaven. Do you believe the saints of the Old Testament are now with Jesus?

Please explain the three heavens. I have heard of the third heaven, but I thought there was only one.

PRAYER 154

Why doesn't God answer my prayers? Is it wrong to pray about every little thing?

What is your opinion on persisting in prayer for lost souls?

What is the sinner's prayer? Does God listen to the prayer of an unbeliever?

What does it mean to pray in Jesus' name? My children are believers but do not study the Word of God. In John 14:14 the Lord says, "If ye shall ask any thing in my name, I will do it." I have prayed so much for them and now wonder if the fault is with me.

SALVATION 162

If the Jews had accepted Jesus Christ as the Messiah, would He still have had to die on the cross for our sins?

I know my sins are taken care of at the cross by Jesus' blood, and His blood will stand judgment for the sins committed after being saved. Can you give Scripture? I know I have grievously failed my Lord many, many times.

I enjoyed your Bible study on 1 Thessalonians 1:3 in which you said that works must follow our profession of faith or it was only a profession. I am disturbed by preaching which implies that people are saved no matter what their lifestyles are like. These preachers don't advocate a wrong lifestyle, but they say the salvation matter is settled. Certainly if the person is sincere, this is true but there ought to be more warning like Paul gave throughout this epistle. What is your opinion?

At this point in my life I don't know how to believe anymore. I really thought in the year 1949 I had received Jesus as my Savior just before my wife left me. Many things happened to me, and I went back to my old ways. How can I be sure I'm saved?

Can a person be born again two times? Please answer. You are my last hope.

I thought I was born again when I was fifteen years old. I felt happy and secure in Christ. But over time, sin surely crept in, and I went the downward path. Three marriages, adultery, lies, drinking. Was I born again? What do I do now?

A person in our church who holds a very responsible position declares we are saved by *love* instead of grace, as stated in Ephesians 2:8, and also, that "according to His *mercy* He has saved us." He says mercy is the undeserved love of God. He also quotes Romans 8:24 and says we are saved by *hope*. Is there anything anywhere that says we are saved by love?

I am quite sure you believe "once saved always saved." But Hebrews 10:26 seems to prove you wrong.

Is the doctrine of eternal security an insignificant thing? Recently our pastor of ten years announced that he once did believe in eternal security but now does not. He says there could come a time when a believer feels that he can get along without God and therefore does not believe. Consequently, he is lost. So he has asked the congregation to come out of the denomination and go independent in order that he might remain as pastor and preach as he sees it.

Please explain Hebrews 2:3 and 2 Peter 3:9. Do these verses mean we could lose our salvation—"How shall we escape" and "longsuffering to usward"?

One teacher on radio said that the unsaved dead will have a second chance when Jesus Christ returns and also that there will be reincarnation. Where is this written in the Bible?

SIN

What is the doctrine of original sin?

What is the unforgivable sin?

What is the sin against the Holy Spirit and how can
I know if I have committed it?

SECTION FOUR: RELIGIOUS ISSUES

CHILDREN: ACCOUNTABILITY AND INNOCENCE

Why is a child acceptable in heaven before the age
of accountability?

What is the age of accountability? I fear for children
nine and ten and younger who have not yet been
saved at the time of the Rapture. To see them left
here in those terrible times seems out of character
with God.

Are children who die in innocence saved? Do they
go to heaven when they die? What references do
you have?

Matthew 18:3 seems to support the idea that a
child's innocence is a standard for righteousness.
But what is the emphasis of verse 6, "these little
ones which believe in me"?

CHURCH

Some churches have elders, others have presbyters.
Some churches have a pastor who's in charge of
everything, others have pastors that just preach and
teach. Which kind of church structure is biblical?

Can a woman be ordained as a pastor of a Christian
church?

Can a man who is divorced and remarried still be
eligible for a position, such as deacon, in the
church leadership? For example, suppose both parties remarry. Would you feel the husband would be
scripturally qualified for consideration to serve as
deacon? If so, under what circumstances?

Is there any Scripture which says a local church should not fellowship with other Christian churches who differ in doctrine, such as baptism, or with churches who are spiritually alive but fellowship with a liberal church?

Please discuss the matter of separation for all true born-again believers from unbelievers regardless of church affiliation.

DEATH: BURIAL METHODS

Should Christians be embalmed or cremated? I have come to feel strongly that both practices desecrate the body and hate to think of it being done to me or to a loved one after death.

OCCULTISM

Someone gave me a book and a deck of tarot cards for a birthday gift. Are they good or bad? Are they sinful?

Can a Christian use astrology? An accurate horoscope has helped me understand people better—their strong and weak points, why they act, think, react as they do, which types are better suited for certain tasks than others. I realize the power of God can override any traits, but is it wrong to be aware of what our human nature is or how it operates?

SABBATH

Was the Sabbath always on Saturday? Why don't we have church on the Sabbath, like the Jews do?

SHROUD OF TURIN

Do you believe the Shroud of Turin is Christ's burial cloth, and why or why not?

SECTION FIVE: SOCIAL ISSUES AND WORLD CONCERNS

ring men's company? And what do you think of
men who wear women's underthings and paint
their faces and nails and wear loud perfumes and
even women's dresses?

Is AIDS God's curse on homosexual behavior?

I am ashamed to go to our pastor to seek help. My
son is a homosexual. I am divorced and remarried
to a fine Christian, and we have a good Christian
marriage which neither of us had before. You have
mentioned that you have received letters from people who were once homosexuals and are no longer.
That is what I want for my son. No one in my family has confronted him about it, yet none of the men
in the family like him or want to be around him.
How can I handle this?

PACIFISM   218

Scripture says to do all things diligently for the
Lord, so how can I put old things of the flesh behind me—like immorality, impure passion, evil
desire, greed, and anger—and then go to war and
kill someone and say I did it in the name of Christ
and His love? Or if someone wants to take advantage of me and persecute me unjustly by stealing
my possessions, and Jesus says give them my shirt
also, how could I kill someone for something that
isn't supposed to matter that much to me?

SELF-DEFENSE   220

Should a Christian defend himself against an intruder? I believe that God would not expect us to
remain idle, but others in my Bible class believe we
shouldn't resist because, they say, there is no Bible
reference to the contrary.

You embarrassed me when you advocated firearms
in the household based on an Old Testament admonition concerning the house as a stronghold. You
seem to forget that you live in a "shoot first and ask
questions later" society, quite the antithesis of what
Christ was all about.

You expressed great sympathy and compassion for the victims of violent crime, which I share. But the Christian is to exercise sympathy and compassion for the criminal also. God loves not only good men but also bad men.

TOBACCO 224

According to the Scriptures, is it a sin to use tobacco?

INTRODUCTION

"First of all, let me apologize for the tardiness of this reply. I've been snowed under. . . ."

Indeed, Dr. J. Vernon McGee was!

As his "Thru the Bible" radio program, which first aired in 1967, gained popularity, the volume of mail he received increased. Thousands of letters from people of all ages and denominations wrote asking questions relating to Bible doctrine, their personal relationships with God, and the way God relates to the world around them:

"I'm afraid I've committed the unforgivable sin. . . . Will God take me back?"

"Must I be baptized to be saved?"

"Did dinosaurs really exist?"

Dr. McGee couldn't ignore the questions from his beloved listeners. They were good questions; they deserved good answers. But how would he manage to respond? With a busy pastorate and an extensive conference ministry, his schedule was already too tight.

A question-and-answer radio program on Saturdays was the solution. Now he didn't have to give clever, concise, inadequate answers. He could lean back in his chair, open his Bible and just talk to these folk, giving them background and illustrations and maybe an anecdote to put it in shoe leather for them.

In this book, you will read some of those answers, gleaned from tape recordings of hundreds of broadcasts over the years. We have abbreviated the questions (some were several pages long), but the answers are virtually as he gave them.

If he were writing this introduction, he would conclude by saying,

It would be a deep disappointment if this volume found its way into a musty library to fill space. My prayer is that it stay at the crossroads of life where the action is!

CHRISTIAN LIFE

BUSINESS

Q. Does 2 Corinthians 6:14 forbid a Christian's working in partnership with a non-Christian?

A. "Be ye not unequally yoked together with unbelievers: for what fellowship hath righteousness with unrighteousness? and what communion hath light with darkness?" (2 Cor. 6:14). Paul here makes an appeal to the Corinthian believers to make a clean break with idolatry, to make a break from the sins of the flesh and the worldliness that is in the world.

In the Old Testament under the Mosaic Law God gave a law to His people who were largely engaged in agriculture. He said that they were not to yoke together an ox and an ass. That would be yoking together unequal animals. One was a clean animal and the other was unclean. Here God is speaking to believers, and He says that the believer should not be yoked together with an unbeliever. How are people yoked together? Well, they are yoked together in any form of real union such as a business enterprise, a partnership, a marriage, a long-term enterprise.

Certainly marriage is the yoking together of two people. An unbeliever and a believer should not marry. A clean animal and an unclean animal should not be yoked together to plow. A child of God and a child of the devil cannot be yoked together and pull together in their life goals.

Another example is identification with an institution. If a man is a professor in a seminary and is conservative and holds the great truths of the Bible but the seminary has gone liberal, such a man should get out of that seminary because he is drawing a salary there and is identified with its work and organization. He is associated with it in a very tangible, real way which makes him unequally yoked with unbelievers.

Suppose, however, that an evangelist comes to town and holds services for one or two weeks. Although he uses certain methods that you would not condone, he is preaching Christ and God is blessing his ministry. Are you to join with him?

Notice how Paul did it. Paul would first go to the synagogue when he entered a new city. Can you imagine a place where there would be more opposition to Jesus Christ than in the synagogue? Yet that is where Paul began. I am not condemning him for it because God led him to do it that way. Now if Paul had *joined* himself to one of those synagogues, become the rabbi and stayed there, then that would have been considered a yoke.

You see, Paul is talking about being yoked together in a permanent arrangement, like marriage, a business partnership, a professorship in a school, or membership in a church. He is talking about yoking ourselves with *unbelievers*, as he makes clear in the next verse: "And what concord hath Christ with Belial? or what part hath he that believeth with an infidel?" (2 Cor. 6:15).

CONSCIENCE

Q. How does the believer differentiate between the work of the Holy Spirit within and the promptings of conscience? Before I was a Christian I listened to and obeyed my conscience. If, as a believer, the Holy Spirit is my guide, do I still need the conscience? What has happened to it?

A. Well, let me say that the conscience is mentioned again and again in the Word of God. There were periods, apparently, in the history of the world, such as the time of Noah, when men followed their consciences. The end of the book of Judges describes a very bad period when man departed from God's revealed law. "Every man did that which was right in his own eyes" (Judges 21:25). And, by the way, we've come to that kind of a situation again today.

The question of the conscience of man has been a subject that philosophers, and now the psychologists, bat around quite a bit. Kant, the great philosopher of the past, denied (or at least he never mentioned) man's having a conscience. He divided man into three parts, but he never mentioned conscience at all. Even when he discussed the section that he calls "the Sensibility of Man" he was not really talking about conscience at all. Obviously, every person is born with a conscience that somehow dictates to him right and wrong. As a person grows older there comes a time when a conscience may be "seared with a hot iron," so that he has no conscience about either right or wrong. I think right now we are in a period when there are many people in this country, and many of our leaders, who have no conscience at all about right or wrong. The moral standards of the past are now being erased, and we are producing a generation that has no conscience about what the Bible calls sin.

When a person trusts Christ he is indwelt by the Holy Spirit and he is to be guided by the Holy Spirit. But how does the Holy Spirit guide the individual? Actually, some folks say you don't need your conscience to guide you. No, I think that just as a conscience can be trained and brought to the place where it is hardened, so it can also be made very sensitive. I am confident that the Holy Spirit works through the conscience of a believer. I have found out in my own life (and that is the only way you can test these things) that many things I did before I was saved, I had no conscience about at all. To me, it wasn't a question of right or wrong. I was doing what I wanted to do. After I was saved I don't think I got rid of my conscience. I think the Holy Spirit began to work through that conscience.

I never shall forget the break I made from a practice I had. (I ought not tell specifically what this recreation was because Scripture does not mention whether it is right or wrong, and Christians are divided on the issue.) But I had engaged in this behavior a great deal. The moment I was saved I began to develop a conscience about it. I decided to break off gradually. And I tell you, a fellow saw me at the place where I don't think I should have been, and he said to me—and he didn't say it very nicely—"This is a hell of a place for a preacher to be!" Well, I came to the conclusion he was right. I got my hat and left, and I never went back again.

I believe that the Spirit of God uses and works through the conscience of a believer today. Also, I think it is possible for an unbeliever to reach the place where his conscience is cauterized from years of violation so that it doesn't work at all for him.

EMOTIONS

Q. May a believer get angry at God? My Sunday school material states that when the writer of Lamentations mourned over the destruction of Jerusalem and the temple, he was expressing anger. I believe, however, that a Christian has no right to become angry at God. But if he does, he had better make sure he gets over it very quickly and asks for forgiveness.

A. I certainly agree with you, and may I say that there is absolutely no scriptural basis permitting a believer to become angry with God. There are many times when the believer does not *understand* what is happening to him and why God has permitted a certain thing to take place. He may even cry out, "Why did You let this happen to me?" But to get angry with God is something that, very frankly, is not permitted for a child of God. A true child of God would never do that.

Remember, God said to Jonah, "Doest thou well to be angry?" And he answered, "I do well to be angry." He was angry that God didn't destroy the Ninevites, but that does not mean in any sense of the word that he was angry with God. He was disappointed in the way God had handled it. The Ninevites were a brutal people, and Jonah wanted them destroyed (see Jonah 3 and 4).

Now let me take up the book of Lamentations. In the first chapter Jeremiah was actually weeping over the city of Jerusalem and what had happened to it. His emotion was not *anger* but *sorrow*. To miss that makes me suspect that the author of the Sunday school literature is possibly a "Christian" psychologist. I have always given the liberals credit for being intelligent, but I have noticed recently in several books that the liberals can be really stupid. They can be as stupid as those of us who are fundamentalists and, believe me, to make the statement that Jeremiah is expressing anger is stupid. He is expressing sorrow, and to miss that is, in my judgment, to miss the entire content of the little book of Lamentations. Now we can all be wrong, but let's not be stupid.

Q. Sometimes I feel lost, that Christ has left me. I really know in my heart He hasn't, but I'm not sure. When you try to live a Christian life and pray to your God, can you tell whether Jesus is always in your life?

A. Well, I think your primary problem is that you are trusting feelings. One day you feel very good, and another day you feel very bad. Now, very frankly, I feel very good today. I felt wretched yesterday. And for that reason I didn't make any tapes for broadcasting. I was just down, that was all. We can't trust our feelings, either when we are up or when we are down. Our salvation rests upon what the

Word of God says: "And this is the record, that God hath given to us eternal life, and this life is in his Son. He that hath the Son hath life; and he that hath not the Son of God hath not life" (1 John 5:11–12).

"He that hath the Son hath life." It's just as simple as that. Do you have Christ? Are you trusting Him? If you are, then you are saved. It may have rained on your parade, but you *know* you trust Christ. Your salvation rests upon what the Word of God has to say—not upon your feelings at all.

I tell the story about the first time I ever flew in a plane. Boy, did we go through a storm! Every minute I was absolutely sure we were going down. Across the aisle from me sat a former pilot who told me he had flown more than fifty missions over Europe during World War II—and there he was asleep! The storm didn't bother him a bit. The plane was as safe for me as it was for him. But while I felt like we were going down, he was asleep. He was accustomed to that type of thing and felt all right. I didn't feel all right, but feelings had nothing to do with the safety of that plane. And, by the way, we did make it. We landed safely, and I thank God for that!

Feelings are very deceiving, but what does your salvation rest upon? It is not dependent on whether you feel Christ is in your life. Again, feelings can't be trusted, and we ought not to rest upon them at all.

Q. I've become so depressed I have considered suicide. I'm afraid I've committed the unforgivable sin. If there is any hope for me, why doesn't God come close to me? Will God take me back again? I want to feel secure.

A. You are looking for feeling, but it is not feeling that you need; it is *facts*. And the facts are that Christ died for your sin. If you've trusted Him, you have been born again and have become a child of God. According to your letter, you have sinned a very grievous sin. But our Lord not only says to you, "Come unto me, all ye that labor and are heavy laden, and I'll rest you" (Matt. 11:28), but He is saying also to you, "If you [Christians] confess your sins, I am faithful and just to forgive your sins and to cleanse you from all unrighteousness" (see 1 John 1:9).

First of all, you ask why God doesn't come close to you. Did you ever notice that while the prodigal son was in the pigpen the father made no move to get to him? The prodigal son left home on his own volition; he had to come home in the same way. You ask why God doesn't move close to you. Who was it that moved away—God or you? *You* moved away. *You* have to come back. You have to come to Him, and you have to believe Him. He says He will forgive you, but you must turn from your sin. If you continue in your sin, certainly you won't have any feeling of satisfaction such as you say you once had when you trusted Christ. Now I think that satisfaction can be restored if you will confess your sin. And to confess your sin means that you agree with God about it—that it *is sin* and that you are going to turn from it. If you are not turning from your sin, you certainly haven't agreed with God. That is no real confession at all. But if you really mean business with God, He has already forgiven you. And if what you say in this letter is accurate, and I think it is, I would say you have already been forgiven.

God will forgive you because He *says* He'll forgive you. Now believe Him; believe God. Trust Him and turn from your sin. That is the only way that you can have sweet peace in this world today.

And now this final word to you. You must remember that there are certain fruits of sin. Sin pays wages, the highest wages being paid today, and it doesn't even belong to a union. Sin pays off, too, and so your body and your mind have been affected by the life that you have lived. You are going to have to recognize that.

I remember years ago when Mel Trotter held meetings in Nashville, Tennessee. After the meeting one night he, my staff, and I went to a place called Candyland. We ordered big ice cream malts, but he ordered just a little carbonated water. Some of the men were kidding him, and he said,

"When God gave me a new heart, He did not give me a new stomach." He had wrecked his stomach with liquor before coming to Christ. God had not given him a new stomach. Today, you are experiencing some of the fruits of sin. You may continue to experience those fruits. But you can certainly have your sins forgiven. You can come back to your Father and have sweet peace in your life if that really is your desire.

Q. What does a person have to do to have contentment in the heart? Or maybe a better way to say it is, how can I have peace of mind and completely get rid of that ever-lingering feeling of insecurity?

A. Well, let me say that your question is not a foolish question. It is one of the best questions that can be asked today.

If you want peace of mind, the Scripture is very clear: "Being justified by faith, we have peace with God through our Lord Jesus Christ" (Rom. 5:1). That present benefit is yours if you can see that by faith in the substitutionary death of Christ you are saved and that God has extended grace to you—not because of merit but because you have a need.

> For when we were yet without strength, in due time Christ died for the ungodly. For scarcely for a righteous man will one die: yet peradventure for a good man some would even dare to die. But God commendeth his love toward us, in that, while we were yet sinners, Christ died for us (Rom. 5:6–8).

You can't save yourself; He has agreed to do it for you. If you can enter into that—believe Christ and rest in Him— then you can have peace of mind.

However, if you mean by "security" that you expect to go through this world wrapped in plastic or packed in cotton, you are entirely wrong. For instance, when you are on a plane and you fly into a storm and the plane begins to wobble up and down, you'd be a very strange individual if you didn't lose a little of your peace and become a little concerned about the situation. And that would be true if you were in a house that was on fire. If you don't get a feeling of insecurity, you are entirely without feeling. But in every situation you can have that deep peace of mind that comes only through Jesus Christ.

> Be careful [anxious] for nothing; but in every thing by prayer and supplication with thanksgiving let your requests be made known unto God. And the peace of God, which passeth all understanding, shall keep your hearts and minds through Christ Jesus (Phil. 4:6–7).

GIVING

Q. I'm a new Christian and I really want to support my church with my tithe. But my husband says we don't have to donate anything, because tithing is Old Testament and Christians aren't under the Law anymore. What do you think?

A. Well, let's look at how it was done in the early church. The motive for their giving is revealed here: "And this they did, not as we hoped, but first gave their own selves to the Lord, and unto us by the will of God" (2 Cor. 8:5).

I am not sure but what a dedication or consecration service ought to always accompany the offering, because, honestly, He is not interested in your gift until He has your heart and your hand. New Testament Christians not only gave themselves to the Lord, but they gave themselves also to the work of the ministry. This is very practical. Paul is careful in this section to make it clear that our giving proves the sincerity of our love (2 Cor. 8:8).

Give yourself to Him and then give yourself to whatever the work is. This is the reason we are never to give grudgingly. This is the reason we are to give always with great joy—hilariously! Why? Because we are giving ourselves to something we believe in with all our hearts. We need to be sold out to the ministry to which we give. My friend, there is nothing as spiritual as an offering. Your gift tells the sincerity of your love. It tells whether your life really belongs to God or not.

"For if there be first a willing mind, it is accepted according to that as a man hath, and not according to that he hath not" (2 Cor. 8:12). Christian giving is not mechanical. Hear me now very carefully. I do not believe that any believer today is under the Old Testament tithe. We are not under the percentage basis at all. Giving is not mechanical. Nowhere in the New Testament does God specify that the believer is to give a tenth of his income. But wait a moment—for some people it may be a tenth, but I honestly believe that for others it ought to be more.

During the Depression I was pastor of a church in Texas. In this town the only people who actually were able to give during the Depression were the doctors and the man who owned the Coca-Cola plant. The man who owned the Coca-Cola plant was a personal friend of mine, and we used to hunt and fish together. He had a big ranch down on the river, and every time we'd go fishing or hunting he would say to me, "Why don't you preach on the tithe?" Finally one day I said, "I'm going to tell you why."

You see, he was giving more than anyone in the church. So I said to him, "Look, I do not think we are under the tithe today. Paul says that as a man is able, so let him give. There are some people here in this town who get only about $1,000 a year now, and they're living on it. I personally believe that God does not ask those families to give a tenth. I don't really think they should. But the man who is making $20,000 a year ought not to give only a tenth, he ought to be giving half." He never did ask me to preach on the tithe after that. He dropped the subject.

My friend, today giving is in proportion to the way God has prospered you and blessed you. "Upon the first day of the week let every one of you lay by him in store, as God hath prospered him, that there be no gatherings when I come" (1 Cor. 16:2).

If you are looking for a standard for giving, here it is: the Lord Jesus Christ Himself. "For ye know the grace of our Lord Jesus Christ, that, though he was rich, yet for your sakes he became poor, that ye through his poverty might be rich" (2 Cor. 8:9). He was rich but He became poor. He came down here and took a place of poverty. Imagine leaving heaven and coming down to this earth to be born in Bethlehem, living in Nazareth, dying on a cross outside the walls of Jerusalem, and being put into the darkness of a borrowed tomb! He was rich but He became poor for you and me.

Q. How should you give money you've set aside as a faith promise? In our church, some feel your faith promise is between you and the Lord and can be sent directly to missionaries, for example. Others insist that a gift must first be given to the church but can be designated by the giver as to where it should be sent.

A. First of all, I never used the faith promise method when I was a pastor. I did not feel that it was the way God wanted me to go. But this doesn't mean that it is not a method God uses, because I believe, frankly, that it is. Many of my friends in the ministry use it very effectively.

Now, to deal specifically with the point you are making, I would say this: If you are in a church that uses the faith promise method, and if you fill out a card and hand it in, you are promising that you will give a certain amount of money during that year. Of course, all of this is on the basis that God is going to bless you in an unusual way; that is, you're going to get more money than you're getting now. It always impressed me that it is sort of like making a deal with God—"If You bless me, I'm going to give it to You." But be that as it may, if you turned in that card to a local church, then that is where you ought to give your faith promise rather than sending it directly to the missionary.

I am sure you have the freedom to give any way you want to give, but when you signed that card, you obligated yourself. If you're going to give that amount, it ought to go through the local church as a matter of common fairness and honest dealing.

NATURE OF MAN

Q. I have understood you to say that we all have the carnal nature, or the "old man" of sin, but that we cannot get rid of it. If that is so, how do you interpret Romans 7:19–25; 8:1–2?

A. To interpret fully the verses you have given me would require a complete exegesis of chapters 7 and 8 plus the context. Now, I can do that on our *Thru the Bible* weekday radio program. I also have books of exegesis on every book of the Bible in which I go into detail, but here I will try to be specific and brief.

There is a wide range of Scriptures that clarifies the two passages you have cited, showing that we as Christians cannot get rid of our old nature (or carnal nature) in this life. The first Scripture, Romans 8:6–8 says,

> For to be carnally minded is death; but to be spiritually minded is life and peace. Because the carnal mind is enmity against God; for it is not subject to the law of God, neither indeed can be. So then they that are in the flesh cannot please God.

This passage of Scripture actually proves and sets before us that you and I have two natures: a spiritual nature and a carnal nature. (If we didn't have the carnal nature, why would Paul write to us about it?) We have a carnal nature. In effect he says, "If you're going to live by that carnal nature, that old nature that you have, it means death as far as service to God is concerned; you couldn't do anything that would please God." Anything that Vernon McGee does in the flesh God hates. He will not have it. He cannot use it. Only that which is done by the power of the Holy Spirit working through the new nature is acceptable to God.

That is Paul's argument in all of these passages that you have cited. He makes it very clear that God has made adequate arrangement for us not to continue in sin, not to live by that old nature, but that we can have a victory over it. Paul says in Romans 6:1–2: "What shall we say then? Shall we continue in sin, that grace may abound? God forbid. How shall we, that are dead to sin [or rather, *we that died*— because we are not dead to sin, we *died* to sin] live any longer therein?" Now, when did we die to sin? More than nineteen hundred years ago when Christ died. He died to pay the *penalty* of our sins, but He did not deliver us from the *presence* of it. Sin is about us today, but He provided a way that we should not live in the *power* of sin. And what Paul is saying, beginning with chapter 6, is that something has to happen to us. We are to know that we were baptized into Christ. And how were we baptized into Christ? The word *baptism* means "identification." We were identified with Him. When Christ died, I died and you died (if you're a Christian); that is, Christ paid the penalty for our sin. And your sin, if you trust Christ, is not out yonder in front of you to be judged; it is back of you on the cross.

Not only that, but you have been raised to newness of life in Christ. He is at God's right hand, and you are in Christ. Now He wants you to live for Him down here. And how are you going to live for Him down here? You are going to have to live by the power of the indwelling Holy Spirit.

You have also cited Romans 8:1–2, which says, "There is therefore now no condemnation to them which are in Christ Jesus, who walk not after the flesh, but after the Spirit."

If you are a child of God, there is no condemnation as far as the judgment of sin; but if you are going to please Him, you are going to have to walk by the Spirit and not by the flesh. Paul says there is a warfare. He speaks of that warfare that went on in his own life (see Rom. 7). What he desired to do he didn't do, and the reason was, he says, "For I know that in me (that is, in my flesh) dwelleth no good thing: for to will is present with me; but how to perform that which is good I find not" (Rom. 7:18). This means that you and I today have an old nature, and God cannot accept it. Believers also have a new nature, but there is no power in that new nature. The power comes from the Spirit of God. "For the law of the Spirit of life in Christ Jesus hath made me free from the law of sin and death" (Rom. 8:2).

The only way you can please God is to live by the power of the Holy Spirit.

PRIESTHOOD OF BELIEVERS

Q. What do you mean when you say, "I am a catholic priest but not a Roman Catholic"?

A. Well, I made that statement when we were studying 1 Peter. I said I am a catholic priest because the word *catholic* means "general" and has to do with anything that is general. Peter speaks of the priesthood of believers, and I belong to that priesthood of believers. You do, too, if you are a believer. Now *Roman* means a specific kind of priest, and it refers to the Roman Catholic Church. Therefore, I'm a catholic priest but not a Roman Catholic priest because, you see, "Roman" is specific and "catholic" is general, and it's pretty difficult to have a specific general or a general specific anything. Using the words literally, every believer is a "catholic" or "general" priest.

Since we belong to Christ, we can come into His presence, into the very holy of holies. Simon Peter tells us: "But ye are a chosen generation, a royal priesthood, an holy nation, a peculiar people; that ye should shew forth the praises of him who hath called you out of darkness into his marvellous light" (1 Pet. 2:9). He is saying several wonderful things about us here.

We are a "chosen generation"; that is, an elect race. Back in the Old Testament God chose Israel as His people. In the Scriptures there are two elect groups of people: the nation Israel, called an elect nation; and the church, called an elect nation and an elect people.

We are "a royal priesthood." In the Old Testament God first of all chose the entire nation of Israel to be His priests. (I believe that in the Millennium the whole nation of Israel will be priests here on this earth.) However, they sinned, and so God chose one tribe out of that nation. The priests came from this one tribe. Today there is no priesthood on the earth which God recognizes except one. Today every *believer* in the Lord Jesus Christ is a priest. Israel *had* a priesthood; today the church *is* a priesthood.

We are "an holy nation." The nation Israel was never holy in conduct, and the same can be said of the church. Israel's failure is glaring; the church's failure is appalling. Yet we are holy in our relationship with Him because *Christ* is our righteousness. If you have any standing before God, it is not in yourself; it is in Christ. I can't think of anything more wonderful than that today I stand complete in Him. What a joy it is to be a member of a holy nation, which is a new nation in the world today.

We are "a peculiar people"—a people of His own. We are a people for acquisition, a people for God's own possession. We belong to Him. Therefore, there is in the world not only a new nation but also a people that belong to Him.

And God calls His own. He calls *you* today, my friend. It doesn't matter who you are or which race you belong to, Jesus Christ is calling to you to be His own. He wants you to join a chosen generation and a royal priesthood. He is not inviting you to wear robes or to recite rituals but to join a priesthood that has access to God.

RELATIONSHIPS

Q. I am against divorce, but I heard a minister say that divorce is all right as long as God didn't join you together in the first place. My Sunday school teacher says every situation is different, and God expects us to use common sense. Would you please comment on both of these views?

A. First of all, let me say this: The instructions given in the Word of God pertain to Christians. One of these men who has family seminars uses the expression (he used it with me the other day), "Save the American home." Well, that sounds great! But he is going to save it by having everyone follow certain Christian rules and regulations.

Did you ever stop to think that in the New Testament there are no instructions given to the unsaved family regarding the running of their home? The instructions in Ephesians 5 are given to believers—not only to believers but to Spirit-filled believers. They are the only ones who can have the experience that is mentioned in that passage. So you have in the Word of God specific instructions to believers.

God hasn't promised to bless the marriage of those in the world at all. Our main purpose is not to get their marriage straightened out but to get them saved. We're not trying today to save the American home; we're trying to save the American individual in the home. And if you get mama saved and papa saved, you might be able to get little Willie saved. And if you get them saved, you have a Christian home and you can talk to them about the kind of life that they should live as believers.

Now let's read what our Lord Jesus said about divorce:

And it came to pass, that when Jesus had finished these sayings, he departed from Galilee, and came into the coasts of Judaea beyond Jordan; and great multitudes followed him; and he healed them there. The Pharisees also came unto him, tempting him, and saying unto him, Is it lawful for a man to put away his wife for every cause? And he answered and said unto them, Have ye not read, that he which made them at the beginning made them male and female, and said, For this cause shall a man leave father and mother, and shall cleave to his wife: and they twain shall be one flesh? Wherefore they are no more twain, but one flesh. What therefore God hath joined together, let not man put asunder. They say unto him, Why did Moses then command to give a writing of divorcement, and to put her away? He saith unto them, Moses because of the hardness of your hearts suffered you to put away your wives: but from the beginning it was not so. And I say unto you, Whosoever shall put away his wife, except it be for fornication, and shall marry another, committeth adultery: and whoso marrieth her which is put away doth commit adultery (Matt. 19:1–9).

These verses need to be examined in light of all other Scripture having to do with divorce. First Corinthians devotes the entire seventh chapter to the subject. "And unto the married I command, yet not I, but the Lord, Let not the wife depart from her husband: but and if she depart, let her remain unmarried, or be reconciled to her husband: and let not the husband put away his wife" (1 Cor. 7:10–11). Here is a commandment. Paul is putting it on the line. The wife is not to leave her husband, and the husband is not to leave his wife. If one or the other is going to leave, then they are to remain unmarried.

There was a new problem which presented itself in Corinth. After Paul had preached the gospel to them, a husband in a family would accept Christ but the wife would not. In another family it might be that the wife would accept Christ and the husband would not. What were the believers to do under such circumstances?

But to the rest speak I, not the Lord: If any brother hath a wife that believeth not, and she be pleased to dwell with him, let him not put her away. And the woman which hath an husband that believeth not, and if he be pleased to dwell with her, let her not leave him. For the unbelieving husband is sanctified by the wife, and the unbelieving wife is sanctified by the husband: else were your children unclean; but now are they holy (1 Cor. 7:12–14).

If one was married to an unsaved man or to an unsaved woman and there were children in the family, Paul said they should try to see it through. Paul says, "Stay right where you are if you can." "For what knowest thou, O wife, whether thou shalt save thy husband? or how knowest thou, O man, whether thou shalt save thy wife?" (1 Cor. 7:16). This should be the goal of the wife. I know several women who were married to unsaved men and tried to win them for Christ. This also should be the goal of the husband who is married to an unsaved woman. Winning them for Christ should be uppermost in their consideration.

"But as God hath distributed to every man, as the Lord hath called every one, so let him walk. And so ordain I in all churches" (1 Cor. 7:17). Paul is advising people to stay in their present situation. They are not to walk out of their marriage after they have heard and accepted the gospel. They are to stay married if the unbelieving partner will allow it.

This ought to answer the question for today. Unfortunately, there are some ministers and evangelists who have advised people who were divorced and remarried to go back to their first mates after they had come to Christ. I can't think of anything more tragic than that kind of advice. I know one woman who finally ended up in a mental institution because she followed the advice of some evangelist who told her to leave her second husband and her lovely Christian home and go back to a drunken husband whom she had previously divorced. How foolish can one be?

Q. I was divorced by my alcoholic, unfaithful husband many years ago. Now a wonderful Christian man has entered my life. Is it all right to marry again?

A. I believe the following Scripture pertains to situations of this nature: "But if the unbelieving depart, let him depart. A brother or a sister is not under bondage in such cases: but God hath called us to peace" (1 Cor. 7:15).

If the unbeliever walks out of the marriage, that is another story. Then the believer is free. Is one free to marry again? I believe that under certain circumstances Paul would have given permission for that. I do not think one can put down a categorical rule either way for today. I think that each case stands or falls on its own merits. I'm afraid this can easily be abused, even by Christians. I am afraid sometimes a husband or a wife tries to get rid of the other and forces the spouse to leave in order to have a "scriptural ground" for divorce. In cases like this I always urge the folk to talk to their pastor who knows them personally and is familiar with the background of the previous marriage relationships.

Q. My fiancé says that we should start sleeping together before we get married so we will have an established relationship when we get married. He says it isn't wrong because we're engaged. What does the Bible say?

A. I'll answer the last part of your question first so we will have God's answer. In the Ten Commandments given by God to His people is this: "Thou shalt not commit adultery." Since your marriage has not taken place, having sex together is adultery.

The request your fiancé has made of you raises two questions about him. First, does he really love you or is he confusing love with lust? Second, is he being honest in promising that he will marry you? In spite of all this new emphasis on sex, the divorce courts continue to grind out their monotonous story of the tragedy of modern marriage in ever-increasing numbers. I think it is time that God is heard. I feel that the pulpit is long overdue in presenting what God has to say on this subject.

In the very beginning it was God who created them

male and female. It was *God* who brought the woman to the man. God blessed them, and marriage became sacred and holy and pure. And, my friend, it is the only relationship among men and women that God does bless down here. He promises to bless no other. He says that if marriage is made according to His plan, He will bless it.

Christian marriage is an adumbration of that wonderful relationship between Christ and the believer. Christian marriage and the relationship of Christ and the church are sacred.

Listen to me very carefully. The physical act of marriage is sacred, a sacrament made by God Himself and one which He sanctifies. He says that this relationship is to reveal to you the love of Christ for your soul. Therefore, the woman is to see in a man one to whom she can yield herself in a glorious abandonment. She can give herself wholly and completely. She can find perfect fulfillment and satisfaction in this man, because this is the man for her and because he has committed himself to her in marriage.

You can have a bargain-basement, second-hand, hand-me-down marriage if you want. If you take the cheap way you will have a home that in no respect will represent Christ and the church. It can be a hell down here; take it from one who has counseled with many couples who are Christians. But, my young person, you can ask God for the best. You can tell Him that you will not accept anything short of the best, and He will give you a life in *living color*. In marriage, sex is a holy relationship. And if it is not, it is no more than an animal act. When a man and a woman give themselves to each other in an act of marital love, they can know the love of Christ as no one else can know it. That is exactly what is said in the Word of God: "This is a great mystery: but I speak concerning Christ and the church" (Eph. 5:32).

When a man and woman come to that place, then they can know Christ who gave Himself *in love* for us. They can know then what it is to offer themselves in total dedication to Him.

God wants His children to be happily married. He has a plan and purpose for every one for us if we would only listen to Him.

SIN AND FORGIVENESS

Q. In John 20:23 Jesus said, "Whosoever sins ye remit, they are remitted unto them; and whosoever sins ye retain, they are retained." How can we do this?

A. What is it that will enable you to be forgiven of your sins? The gospel, that is, the good news of the death and resurrection of Christ. I have no power and no one else has any power to say to another, "You are forgiven." Only the Lord Jesus Christ was able to say, even to that woman who was taken in adultery, "Neither do I condemn you." But He also told her to go and sin no more, indicating that what she had done was sin, and He alone could forgive sin.

The Lord Jesus told Peter, and He meant it for all the apostles, "I am giving to you the keys of the kingdom." The symbolism was understood by them because in their day the scribes carried at their waist keys that were symbolic of their office. They were regarded as the only ones who could unlock the Scriptures. So today how can you and I remit sins? By telling them the gospel! That is the most glorious privilege in the world!

Q. Would you please differentiate between faults and sins? You have said we should confess our *faults* to one another but our *sins* to God. So many faults and sins overlap one another. Is there a line that can be drawn?

A. My answer is no, I don't think you can draw a line between certain things. There are faults in sins and sins in faults. When they do overlap, you have a two-way confession to make. If you have harmed somebody and there has been a sin against God as well, then you will make that thing right as far as the individual is concerned, and you will also make confession to God. I think that each individual would have to determine that for himself.

For example, a fault would be that you misrepresented something concerning an individual. When I was pastor in downtown Los Angeles, someone brought me word concerning a preacher friend of mine. It was a lie if there ever was a lie, but I did not realize it at the time. So I quoted it to a mutual friend, saying I was distressed to hear this about our friend. He said, "Well, I don't believe it." I responded, "It's hard for me to believe it, but this man seemed to know what he was talking about." Our friend went to the preacher and told him about it. The preacher called me and wanted to know if he could have lunch with me. During our lunch he told me the background of this incident. When he explained it all, it was obvious this other man had absolutely misrepresented it, so I confessed to him. Also, I called the other man to whom I had told it, told him I was wrong about it and confessed to him. In my prayer the next morning I said to the Lord that I regretted repeating that rumor and asked that He would help me not make statements like that. Now that was a *fault*—I didn't deliberately lie.

There have been times when I have deliberately lied. You probably didn't think I would do that, but I have. I have regretted it afterward and confessed it only to the Lord because the lie did not affect anyone or have anything to do with anyone's reputation, nor did it give out false information. It was between the Lord and me.

I don't think you could differentiate by classifying one thing a fault and another thing a sin. Rather, classify it according to your relationship to God. Ask yourself, *How does this affect my relationship to God?* If it involves an individual down here, you would want to go to the person and make the thing right.

You remember that Zacchaeus, who had wronged many people, said, "If I have taken anything by false accusation, I'll restore it fourfold." But he also needed the forgiveness of God (see Luke 19:1–10).

And you remember David in his great sin recognized

that it was against God, saying in Psalm 51:4: "Against thee, thee only, have I sinned." But also he had certainly committed against others a terrible sin that he needed to rectify. And I believe that as far as David was able, he did rectify his sin. There is a two-way confession to make when there is any question about it.

I think that there are other sins that should not be confessed to individuals and certainly not publicly. My feeling is that there has been too much of this public confession of sin which should be taken care of privately with the Lord. If you have taken care of it privately with the Lord, then you should not get up before a group and make a long testimony, gloating over your sins! I hear too much of that today. Your relationship to God and your relationship to the injured party are the things that should enter into your confession.

Q. Is there Scripture to prove that a living body in the Spirit can live without sin?

A. Well, I think it was Dr. C. I. Scofield who used to put it like this: "God has made every arrangement for us to live without sin, but," he added, "I never met anybody like that." I agree with Dr. Scofield. The basis for making that statement is, of course, found in 1 John 2:1: "My little children, these things write I unto you, that ye sin not." God has made every arrangement so that we can live without sin, but He adds this: "And if any man sin, we have an advocate with the Father, Jesus Christ the righteous."

Although God has made ample and adequate provision for us not to sin, our entrance into His provision is imperfect because of our imperfection. Notice that this verse does not say that we *cannot* sin, but John is writing to us that we *may not* sin. God wants us to walk in a manner that is well pleasing to Him; that is, He wants us to walk in obedience to His Word.

Let me say again that I have never met anyone who lived without sinning. I've met some who thought they had reached that grandiose plane, but they hadn't impressed the people around them that they were sinless. And God isn't impressed either; back up one verse to 1 John 1:10: "If we say that we have not sinned, we make him a liar, and his word is not in us." That is pretty plain, isn't it!

SUICIDE

Q. I was completely surprised when one of my friends from church committed suicide. How could a Christian kill himself?

A. Now a Christian is a person who has accepted Christ and has been born again by the Spirit of God, indwelt by the Spirit of God. That cannot be changed at all. That Christian can get into sin as the prodigal son did, but he can always go home.

How can a *Christian* commit suicide? That *is* a sin, and somebody points out that they don't have time to ask for forgiveness. Well, I think there are many Christians who die with unconfessed sins. They are going to have to settle them at the judgment seat of Christ. Paul, you remember, said if we would judge ourselves, we would not be judged. Certainly a suicide wouldn't have much of a chance to confess. However, I can understand that a Christian may think he has gotten into a situation where there is no way out. He gets so down that he turns to suicide as the only alternative he can see.

And I can understand that a Christian might have a mental breakdown, a catastrophic illness, or certain other things which might cause him to do this. I would not sit in judgment upon a professing Christian who does this because, to begin with, the minute he commits this act he is out of your hands and out of my hands. We cannot pass judgment on him. And I do know this: if that person is a child of God, he is saved. I don't care what you say, he is *saved* if he is a child of God.

Let me tell you a story about an encounter during my

first pastorate. I was sitting on the front porch one summer day in a rocking chair, which I like to do, and all of a sudden a man appeared at the end of the porch—he'd come down the alleyway—and sat down on the edge of the porch. Then he took out a great big, rusty revolver, laid it down, and said to me, "If you can't give me a good reason why I shouldn't kill myself, I'm going to commit suicide."

Well, that took me aback. I didn't know what to say at first, but I began to talk to the young man. I said to him, "I'll tell you what. If you can show me that you would solve your problems by taking your life, I'd be willing to get you a better gun than you've got there so you can do a better job of it." I continued, "You don't solve your problem by taking your life; you merely complicate and multiply your problem."

So many today think suicide is the way out. Well, that's not the way out. The Lord Jesus told a young man who had asked Him to tell his brother to divide his inheritance with him, "Man, who made Me a judge over you?" Christ is not your judge here, but I want to tell you, when you get over there, He's going to be your judge. And, according to Rev. 20:11–15, it would be well to get matters settled here before you go before the judgment bar of God, the Great White Throne. Even a Christian going before the judgment seat of Christ ought to get things squared away down here before he stands there (2 Cor. 5:10). Suicide will not solve anybody's problems at all!

TEMPTATION

Q. Does God tempt man? I have always believed James 1:13 and have quoted it to myself. But Luke 11:4 hit me like a rock one day. Would you explain "lead me not into temptation"?

A. James 1:13 reads like this: "Let no man say when he is tempted, I am tempted of God: for God cannot be tempted with evil, neither tempteth he any man."

Now, here is a place where there is a distinction without a difference. And this, of course, is a great axiom of the Word of God—that God never tempts anyone with evil; that is not God's way of testing. We sometimes think that the Lord may test us with presenting evil to us; He does not.

Let's look at Luke 11:4: "And forgive us our sins; for we also forgive every one that is indebted to us. And lead us not into temptation; but deliver us from evil." The whole point here is "lead us not into *testing.*" I do not know about you, but I do not want God to test me. I believe that He permitted me to have cancer to test me. I'm sure of that. But I want to say this to you, I pray now, "Lead me not into that kind of testing again, deliver me from cancer." I prayed that prayer this morning, that God would keep me well and not let there be a recurrence of cancer. And I have multitudes of friends out there who also pray that prayer. I think that's in keeping with what the Lord Jesus said, "Lead me not into testing." And then, "If I fall into evil, deliver me from it."

James is saying something altogether different. He says that God doesn't test you with evil. You might want to raise the question about whether cancer is evil or not. It's evil, but not in a moral sense. God does not test you with moral evil.

Most of us are tested when we ourselves get careless about our relationship with God. James continues, "But every man is tempted, when he is drawn away of his own lust, and enticed" (v. 14). It's like the little boy whom his mother heard in the kitchen. She called, "Willie, where are you?" He said, "I'm in the pantry." She said, "What are you doing?" He said, "I'm fighting temptation." Well, the pantry is the wrong place for a little boy to fight the temptation to keep his hand out of that cookie jar. And that is true of us. Many of us fall because we are in the wrong place. Let me put it this way: There's only one place where you can go over Niagara Falls, and that's at Niagara Falls. Likewise, the only place that you can be tempted is in the place of temptation. And it might be well to avoid that place.

I remember a man in Nashville who was wonderfully saved as an alcoholic. In the days of prohibition he knew where every bootlegger in town was located. He told me, "I always made a wide circle around those fellows after I was converted." In other words, he stayed away from the place of temptation. He said, "I always avoid them, and I know where they are, too."

The Life of Christ

TEACHINGS

Q. Please explain Luke 13:18-21, the parable of the mustard seed and the leaven. Why does it say, "The kingdom of God . . . is like . . ."?

A. May I say to you, here is a place where you ought to put together all four Gospels. In the Gospel of Matthew you have, in chapter 13, the mystery parables. Matthew makes the question very clear. Jesus presented the kingdom of heaven as being at hand. Well, what is going to happen to it now, with Jesus crucified and gone back to heaven?

These mystery parables reveal a picture of the kingdom of heaven's condition. In the parable of the net there are good fish and bad fish. What you have is a picture of Christendom—a picture of the world as it is today, and the church is in the world.

There is the bad and the good today. In the parable of the yeast when leaven (typifying evil) is hidden in the meal (which depicts the Word of God) that represents false teaching in the church. And there is a great deal of false teaching today.

In the parable of the mustard seed a little bitty seed that wasn't intended to become a great tree got into good soil and became a tree, and the birds rested in it. In the first parable of the sower the birds represent Satan. The symbolism hasn't changed. So here the birds are Satan getting into the tree; the tree, I think, represents the church in the world today, which has become a big organization. Like the church of Laodicea, there is a lot of evil in it. The hard fact is that the devil gets into the church.

Q. What did Jesus mean when He said not to cast your pearls before swine?

A. Jesus used that expression in the Sermon on the Mount (Matt. 7:1–6). He started by saying, "Judge not, that ye be not judged." He didn't say that you are going to be judged by *God* with the kind of judgment with which you judge other folk, but rather that if you are a critic of other people, constantly sitting in judgment on others, then you will be judged to be or known as that kind of person.

Jesus then gave a series of talks. He said, "Thou hypocrite, first cast out the beam out of thine own eye; and then shalt thou see clearly to cast out the mote out of thy brother's eye" (v. 5). Don't be trying to take a mote (or speck) out of somebody else's eye when you've got a beam (or log) in your own. The contrast, of course, is that you are judging some little thing in someone else, whereas you may be guilty of things far more serious. For instance, maybe you say "This Miss So-and-so uses too much lipstick." Well, that is a very small item, and maybe she needs that much. But you judge her for that. Well, may I say to you, this business of gossip is worse than using lipstick. And sitting in judgment is much worse, so you have the beam in your eye and she has the mote in hers.

Then our Lord goes on to say, "Give not that which is holy unto the dogs" (v. 6). Now among the Jews, the Gentiles were known in that day as dogs. Israel didn't have a very high estimation of Gentiles! Jesus continued, "Neither cast ye your pearls before swine, lest they trample them under their feet, and turn again and rend you." This may be a little difficult to interpret, but I think the Lord meant it like this: "You are wasting your time witnessing to certain people." Now that may seem very strange to you; but there are times, there are situations, when it is worthless for you to attempt to witness.

Let me give you an example. When I was pastor in Nashville, there was a man whom I had known when I worked in the bank. He had become an alcoholic, and his wife was getting ready to leave him. But he was a man who had gained some prominence—he had been elected to the state legislature. Then he had a wonderful conversion.

Coming out of Murfreesboro one night, he saw a tent of an evangelist and he stopped. He was about half drunk then, and he was on his way to Nashville to get a room in a hotel. Actually, he intended to commit suicide because his wife said she had had enough and was going to leave him. Well, he went into that tent, sat in the back, and went to sleep. He was pretty well known to the people in the town, and several were interested in him; so after the service they sobered him up. Then the evangelist talked with him, presented the gospel to him, and he was soundly converted. It was a tremendous change! He never tasted another drop from that day to the present.

But when the news of his conversion got back to the legislature, his fellow congressmen began to kid him. He was known for the fun and kidding that he had carried on when he was in the legislature, so the minute he walked in, they said, "Here comes deacon So-and-so." Finally somebody said, "Preach us a sermon!" And others gave out the same cry. They were making quite a bit of it. The moderator rapped for order but couldn't get it. Finally this fellow stood to his feet, and all he said was this: "My Lord told me not to cast my pearls before swine," and he sat down. May I say to you, that was the best use of the passage of Scripture that I have ever heard. These godless legislators were merely kidding him; they did not want to hear the gospel. They were not interested in it at all. They were ridiculing him and the stand that he had taken. There are times when you should not witness at all.

There was a woman who got in the habit of calling me on the phone, and she always called me when she was drunk. We had to get an unlisted telephone number to get rid of her because she would call and want to talk religion with me. She would never call me when she was sober. So the last time that she called (and I knew that our telephone number would be changed) I said, "Look, when you sober up and you want to talk religion, you come down to the church and sit in the pew and you'll hear all the religion that you'll be able to take in at one time." And to my surprise that woman finally came down to the church! I learned that she actually owned a bar—that is, her husband had owned the bar, and when he died she had inherited it. She got rid of it after she was saved, and she became a real witness for the Lord. But I think I would have wasted my time talking to a dead-drunk woman on the telephone about the things of the Lord. Now that's the way I interpret casting your pearls before swine.

Q. In Luke 16:1–9, is Jesus recommending dishonesty to prove His point?

A. Before making any comments, let's read Luke 16:1–8:

And he said also unto his disciples, There was a certain rich man, which had a steward; and the same was accused unto him that he had wasted his goods. And he called him, and said unto him, How is it that I hear this of thee? give an account of thy stewardship; for thou mayest be no longer steward. Then the steward said within himself, What shall I do? for my lord taketh away from me

QUESTIONS AND ANSWERS

the stewardship: I cannot dig; to beg I am ashamed. I am resolved what to do, that, when I am put out of the stewardship, they may receive me into their houses. So he called every one of his lord's debtors unto him, and said unto the first, How much owest thou unto my lord? And he said, An hundred measures of oil. And he said unto him, Take thy bill, and sit down quickly, and write fifty. Then said he to another, And how much owest thou? And he said, An hundred measures of wheat. And he said unto him, Take thy bill, and write fourscore. And the lord commended the unjust steward, because he had done wisely: for the children of this world are in their generation wiser than the children of light.

I want to deal with this part before we read the ninth verse. Our Lord gave certain parables that are not as simple as others. Some, like this one, have a very clever and tremendous meaning.

The story concerns a rich man who has a steward, and the steward has been dishonest in his dealings. While he is still steward he wants to make friends with the people who owe his master; so he calls them in and offers them a big discount if they will pay their bills immediately. Now this will provide friends who will return the favor when he loses his job. He'll be able to step into this man's place of business and say, "Since I gave you a 50 percent discount, would you loan me about 50 drachma?" The Lord Jesus commends this man for his cleverness in using the things in this world. Actually, he is being a crook, but he is following the standards of this world. Our Lord is commending him because he is using his stewardship for his own advantage. He is smart and clever in using his stewardship, but he is crooked. Now listen to our Lord make the application. "And I say unto you, Make to yourselves friends of the mammon of unrighteousness; that, when ye fail, they may receive you into everlasting habitations" (v. 9).

He says in effect to His disciples, "You as the children of light can be clever in using your money for the Lord's work." Here is one of the greatest teachings, I think, that the Lord gave. He says that the people of this world are wiser than the children of light because they use money to promote themselves. They are crooked, they are using the standards of the world, and they would be commended today in business. How many places today go bankrupt and the owner sells at a discount to satisfy the creditors in order that he might have something left for himself? There's a question about whether it's honest or not, but it is the standard of the world.

Now Jesus says, "The children of this world use their money wisely." How about you? I know that God's children are not wise in the way they are using God's money. There are religious rackets actually making money today. Many of God's children are moved by emotion. They see a picture of a little baby who is about to starve to death, and they give without knowing how much of that money (if any) is going to take care of that little baby. They don't check out the organization. How many people today, even in church, hear a plea and give their money without any investigation? Don't you know that the same man who gave generously on Sunday to something he had not investigated, on Monday, when the stock market opened, did not buy a certain stock until he had carefully investigated it? He found out about the management of the company. He found out about how they were conducting their business. He found out whether they were making money or not before he would invest his money with them.

The children of light ought to be smarter. There's not much smart money among Christians. I gasp sometimes when I find out how much some people are giving to certain questionable organizations and churches. Do you *know* it is being used for God's work? Do you *know* it is promoting the cause of Christ? Do you think the Word of God is going out to the world through these organizations? Investigate!

MIRACLES

Q. What was the purpose of the miracle at the wedding at Cana? You've said Mary wanted Jesus to clear her name when she turned to Him and said, "They have no wine" (John 2:3). Had Mary's thoughts been for selfish gain, where would glory have been manifest that day?

A. Well, probably I ought to deal with several questions you have raised regarding that passage in John 2. Verse 11 says, "This beginning of miracles did Jesus in Cana of Galilee, and manifested forth his glory; and his disciples believed on him." Now the purpose of this miracle was, first of all, to convince His disciples who He was. It was not a public miracle at all, but it was done in a small, intimate gathering—a wedding, and a wedding apparently among friends. This is the first miracle that our Lord performed.

Now I think that you need to put yourself in Mary's position. She did not know what He was going to do. She knew what He *could* do, but when He manifested forth His glory, it was for His disciples, and we need to understand that very clearly.

Since it was not a public miracle, I don't think her motive would be selfish if she wanted Him to clear her name. You see, the moment that Mary said to the angel Gabriel, "Behold the handmaid of the Lord," she passed under a cloud. We know this from Psalm 69:12: "They that sit in the gate speak against me; and I was the song of the drunkards." Apparently, down at the corner saloon they made fun of Him and His mother, and she wanted Him to clear her name. I'm not going into detail here, but it fills in part of the silent years in the life of our Lord—what He must have gone through and what Mary went through.

Now why would she want Him to perform a miracle there? She said to Him, "They have no wine." Obviously she intended for Him to do something about it. How could He do anything about it? Well, if my mother had asked me that question, I'd have said, "Do you think that I can make wine out of *water*?" Of course I couldn't, but Mary knows that Jesus can, and so she says to Him, "They lack wine," knowing that here's an opportunity for Him to demonstrate who He is. I believe that is her thought and intent. But He makes it clear to her when He says, "Woman . . . mine hour is not yet come" (John 2:4). But that hour did come! His resurrection proves who He is. Don't forget that the resurrection proves the virgin birth of Jesus Christ.

In Acts 1:14, Luke is very careful to let you know that when they gathered in an upper room before the Day of Pentecost, Mary was there. There must have been a broad smile on her face as she looked from one to the other, and I think she could have said to Simon Peter, "Simon Peter, I told you He was virgin born!"

SINLESSNESS

Q. I heard a TV minister and singer say that Jesus could have sinned while He was here on earth. How could this be possible?

A. Let me say that it was impossible for Jesus to sin. In Luke 1:35, Mary was told, "that holy thing" that will be conceived by the Holy Spirit is the Son of God. He was "holy, harmless, undefiled," and "separate from sinners" (Heb. 7:26). It is rank heresy to say that Jesus Christ could sin or that He had any sin in Him. He was in all points like we are, except for sin. He was not a sinner; He was not contaminated with sin.

Q. How could Psalm 69:5, which refers to the speaker's sin and foolishness, refer to Christ? How can we answer someone who says, "Since verses 4, 7, and 9 speak of Christ, then verse 5 must also refer to Him"?

A. If somebody should come along with that question, I think you have a very good answer for him: verse 5 does refer to Christ. There is no reason to think otherwise. Psalm 69, which is an imprecatory psalm, speaks of the judgment of God. Also, it is a messianic psalm, a psalm that refers to the Lord Jesus Christ.

> *They that hate me without a cause are more than the hairs of mine head: they that would destroy me, being mine enemies wrongfully, are mighty: then I restored that which I took not away. O God, thou knowest my foolishness; and my sins are not hid from thee* (vv. 4–5).

You say, well, how in the world can all that refer to Him? The word translated *foolishness* could also be translated "weakness." "Thou knowest my weakness and my sins are not hid from thee." And someone asks, "'My sins'? How could that be?" Well, 2 Corinthians 5:21 says, "For he hath made him to be sin for us, who knew no sin." He was wounded for our transgressions, as Isaiah 53 makes very clear. He took our sins. He was "a man of sorrows, and acquainted with grief" (v. 3).

And someone says, "He was a very sorrowful individual." No, He wasn't. He was a happy Christ. You need to read *all* of it. "Surely He hath borne our griefs, and carried our sorrows" (v. 4). He didn't have any griefs and sorrows of His own, He had no sin of His own. He was carrying ours. He was actually made sin for us—not in some academic way, but in reality. He was made sin for us.

In Psalm 69 He was crying out to God: "Thou knowest my foolishness," that is, "my weakness." He was weak, He was bowed down. He fell under the weight of that cross. "My sins are not hid from thee." God judged Him there on the cross. Isaiah 53:10 says "it pleased the Lord to bruise Him," that the Lord has put Him to grief. So Psalm 69:5 refers to Christ.

TEMPTATION

Q. If Jesus could not sin, why was He tempted? Why was He put in the wilderness and tested?

A. Jesus was not tempted to see if He *would* fall. He was tempted to show that He *could not* fall. These temptations that came to Him are the temptations that come to us. But He did not fall because He *could* not fall.

And somebody says, "Wait a minute, then He wasn't tempted as we are." He was tempted greater than we ever were tempted. You know, a boat out in the water can stand just so much pressure. As that pressure builds up the boat will finally give way, and when it does then the pressure is relieved. When pressure is put on us, we finally give way and yield to the temptation. That is common knowledge, of course, and we live in a mean world today. Folk put temptation in the presence of a man who is very honorable and in front of some chaste, marvelous woman. They keep building up the pressure because they know there will come a time and a circumstance when those people will probably yield to it.

Now the devil put all the pressure on the Lord Jesus that was possible to put on any creature, and the Lord Jesus withstood it. He could bear all that pressure. So He has been tempted lots more than you and I have. He *really* knows what it is to be tempted. You and I know what it is to be tempted and fall; He did not experience that.

TRIUMPHAL ENTRY

Q. According to the Gospel of Mark, Jesus rode into Jerusalem on a donkey on which no man had ever sat. I know nothing about horses, mules, or donkeys, but since He rode on an unbroken donkey, wouldn't that make this a miracle?

A. Of course it is an assumption that if anybody else had ridden this little donkey, he would have been bucked off. The very fact that Jesus was who He was caused the little animal to be very docile, as if already broken. So I would go along with you that a miracle may be what we have here, although it can't be proven.

LAST SUPPER

Q. What is the significance of communion? Is it really the body and blood of Jesus?

A. Let's look at John 6:

> Verily, verily, I say unto you, He that believeth on me hath everlasting life. I am that bread of life. Your fathers did eat manna in the wilderness, and are dead. This is the bread which cometh down from heaven, that a man may eat thereof, and not die. I am the living bread which came down from heaven: if any man eat of this bread, he shall live for ever; and the bread that I will give is my flesh, which I will give for the life of the world (John 6:47–51).

He came down to this earth—"the Word was made flesh" (John 1:14). He went to the cross to lay down that human life as a sacrifice to pay for your sins and my sins. Friend, when you partake of that, when you *accept* that, you are saved. Someone may say, "Oh, that's so vivid and so strong." That's what they said in that day too. "The Jews therefore strove among themselves, saying, How can this man give us his flesh to eat?" (John 6:52). They were thinking of His literal flesh, of course. "Then Jesus said unto them, Verily, verily, I say unto you, Except ye eat the flesh of the Son of man, and drink his blood, ye have no life in you" (John 6:53). That means to partake of Him spiritually, which is more real than a physical partaking.

> Whoso eateth my flesh, and drinketh my blood, hath eternal life; and I will raise him up at the last day. For my flesh is meat indeed, and my blood is drink indeed. He that eateth my flesh, and drinketh my blood, dwelleth in me, and I in him. As the living Father hath sent me, and I live

*by the Father: so he that eateth me, even he shall
live by me. This is that bread which came down
from heaven: not as your fathers did eat manna,
and are dead: he that eateth of this bread shall
live for ever* (John 6:54–58).

Friend, this is an amazing statement. Our Lord is preparing these men for that Last Supper and the institution of
the Lord's Supper. This, obviously, is something that is not
to be taken literally because He was right there among them.
He is not saying for them to begin to eat Him and to drink
His blood! What He is saying is that He is going to give His
life. In the Upper Room He made it very clear that the blood
is the symbol of life. "For the life of the flesh is in the blood"
(Lev. 17:11). God had taught the Israelites that truth from
the very beginning when He called them out of the land of
Egypt. There at Mount Sinai Moses gave them this great axiom, "the life of the flesh is in the blood," which is also
medically true, by the way. The life of the flesh *is* in the
blood. And Jesus is giving His life. He will shed His blood
upon the cross in giving His life. Salvation comes by ac-
cepting and receiving Him in a most intimate way.

This is the basis for the sacrament of the Lord's Supper.
Friend, there has been just as much disagreement among
believers in the churches down through the ages over the
interpretation of the Lord's Supper as there has been over
baptism. I don't think they have fought over it quite as
much, but the disagreement is there.

Hoc est meus corpus—"This is my body." When He
gave them the bread at the supper in the Upper Room, He
said, "This is my body" (Luke 22:19). Now this statement
has been emphasized in many different ways.

The Roman Catholic Church puts the emphasis upon
this—"*This* is my body." They say that transubstantiation
takes place, that the bread becomes the flesh of Christ. Well,
I don't think our Lord taught cannibalism in any form,
shape, or fashion. This is a wrong emphasis.

Then there are those who have taken the position of the

Lutheran church, which is consubstantiation. This means that by, with, in, through, and under the bread you get the body of Christ. Again, may I say, I think that falls short of what our Lord really means.

Then there are those who take Zwingli's position. This Swiss Reformation leader gave it a spiritual interpretation— it was just a symbol, just a religious ritual, and that is all. I think that most of Protestantism adheres to this interpretation today. Frankly, I feel that falls as far short of the interpretation of the Lord's Supper as the other two do.

Calvin put the emphasis on is—"This is my body." The Reformed faith has always put the emphasis there, as did the early church. The bread is bread, and it always will be bread. It cannot be changed. The wine is always just what it is, and there is no miracle that takes place. You don't get the body of Christ by going through the ritual. And yet, it is more than a ritual.

I had a seminary professor who taught us that in the Lord's Supper it is bread in your mouth, but it is Christ in your heart. Friend, I believe that there is a spiritual blessing that comes in observing the Lord's Supper. I think that He ministers to you spiritually through your obedience in observing the Lord's Supper. There is no hocus-pocus there. Nor is it just an idle ritual. It is meaningful and has a spiritual blessing for the heart. I think that is what our Lord is saying here. An intimate, real relationship with Him is the important thing. When the Israelites ate manna in the wilderness, it was only a temporary arrangement. Jesus has something that is eternal—life which is eternal. We are told at the beginning of this gospel, "In him was life; and the life was the light of men" (John 1:4).

> These things said he in the synagogue, as he taught in Capernaum. Many therefore of his disciples, when they had heard this, said, This is an hard saying; who can hear it? When Jesus knew in himself that his disciples murmured at it, he said unto them, Doth this offend you? What and if ye

shall see the Son of man ascend up where he was
before? It is the spirit that quickeneth; the flesh
profiteth nothing: the words that I speak unto you,
they are spirit, and they are life (John 6:59–63).

There was definite reaction and differences of opinion
to what Jesus had said. Jesus tells them that they are not
going to eat Him literally because He is going back to
heaven. It is the Spirit that makes alive; the flesh profits
nothing. So obviously, friend, He is not talking about His
literal body.

We are to appropriate the Lord's Supper by faith. The
juice in the cup is sweet, and I always taste the sweetness,
remembering that He bore the bitter cup for me on the cross
so that I might have this sweet cup. That sweet cup is to
remind me that He shed His blood for me, and there is a
spiritual blessing there.

"The words that I speak unto you, they are spirit, and
they are life." During my ministry I have always read to the
congregation from the Word of God during the Lord's Supper. I find that the Word of God ministers to the hearts of
people. Why? Because the words of the Lord Jesus are spirit
and they are life.

Q. You seem to bypass John 13:14 in your preaching, so I
wonder what you think about foot washing. What
was the significance of Christ's washing the disciples' feet?

A. I do not bypass it. I have a sermon titled "Is Jesus Still
in the Foot-washing Business?" which deals with the
episode of the Lord Jesus washing the feet of the disciples in
the Upper Room. In John 13:14 the Lord Jesus says, "If I
then, your Lord and Master, have washed your feet; ye also
ought to wash one another's feet." Now I see nothing wrong
in that as a ceremony. I find there are many fine churches
and groups that practice foot washing, and certainly it is in
keeping with the Word of God.

But did the Lord Jesus intend it to mean more than a

physical act? Doesn't it speak of something spiritual? I'm sure it does, because when Jesus came to wash Simon Peter's feet, you remember that Simon Peter at first forbade Him to do so. And our Lord told Simon Peter, "What I do thou knowest not now; but thou shalt know hereafter" (v. 7). Now that is a strange thing to say if all He is doing is washing feet. There is a meaning there that Simon Peter missed. "So after he [Jesus] had washed their feet, and had taken his garments, and was set down again, he said unto them, Know ye what I have done to you?" (v. 12). I'm sure if Simon Peter had answered, he'd have said, "Sure I know, you washed our feet." But there's something more to it. Jesus said in verse 17: "If ye know these things, happy are ye if ye do them." Do what things, wash feet? That would have been obvious, but He said, "*If* ye know them," implying there is a spiritual meaning here.

Well, what did it mean when Jesus washed the feet of His disciples? He and His disciples had come in from the outside with their sandals on, and there was not a servant there to do the customary washing, so the Lord Jesus performed this courtesy. But Jesus kept indicating something more. And today at this moment, He is still in the foot-washing business, up yonder at God's right hand. And how does He wash feet? "If we confess our sins, he is faithful and just to forgive us our sins, and to cleanse us from all unrighteousness" (1 John 1:9). When a believer sins he could go and confess his sin to the Lord. And if he gets cleaned up, he won't be getting back in the pigpen, you can be sure of that. Only pigs like pigpens; sons want to go home and get cleaned up. And that's the difference between a child of God and a child of the devil.

Therefore what Jesus is saying here is simply, "If I then, your Lord and Master, have washed your feet; ye also ought to wash one another's feet" (John 13:14). Well, how are we to do that? Paul makes it very clear to us in Galatians 6:1 where he says, "Brethren, if a man be overtaken in a fault, ye which are spiritual, restore such an one in the spirit of meekness; considering thyself, lest thou also be tempted." Now here is something that I think is tremendous. What does it mean to wash the feet of your brethren? It means that when a brother gets dirty feet, you'll want to go over and wash them. That is, you're going to try to restore him—the Greek word *restore* pictures setting a bone—getting him back in place where he is in fellowship with God and with believers again. I understand this to be the spiritual meaning of foot washing.

GARDEN OF GETHSEMANE

Q. In Luke 22:44 we are told that in the Garden of Gethsemane the Lord's "sweat was as it were great drops of blood." Was He actually sweating blood? I have heard some say His sweat was *like* big drops of blood, but not blood.

A. The language may seem a little cloudy to you, but in the original Greek it seems very clear that His sweat was blood. I think we need to understand it that way.

I recognize there are those who are probably trying to eliminate blood redemption. Blood is not an aesthetic subject, by the way. At the sight of blood some people are made sick, nauseated. As a dowager said one time to a new preacher in Philadelphia, "I hope that you are not going to make too much of the blood. It's very repulsive to me." When he said to her, "Oh, I'm not going to make too much of the blood," she was relieved—until he added, "I *cannot* make too much of the blood."

And I would say that is the thing that a great many people would like to do, eliminate the blood. But you can't eliminate it. Without the shedding of blood there is no remission of sins (see Heb. 9:22). And I think that the language here is clear. The agony of our Savior was so intense that He sweat great drops of blood.

Q. Some believe Jesus was praying to see if there were some other way instead of going to the cross. But since this had been planned by Jesus and the Father, and He came to bear our sins that we might be saved, then it would seem He would know there was no other way for us to be saved except by the cross. So why would He try to find another way?

A. This is not quite the interpretation that is given by those who accept that viewpoint. They say the reason He wanted to avoid the cross was that in His humanity His entire being rebelled against it because He was holy, harmless, undefiled, separate from sinners. The most terrible thing was not the physical suffering, but that He was to be made sin for us—not in an academic way but actually *made* sin. And it was because it was so terrible and horrible that He prayed. Now may I say to you, there is some substance in that viewpoint.

The fact is that the Scriptures have not given us the whys and wherefores. Although we don't understand all that transpired in the Garden that night, we are given enough information to stand on the fringe and worship the One who loved us and gave Himself for us.

Q. What did Jesus mean when He asked in the Garden of Gethsemane, "Let this cup pass from me"? I have always believed Jesus' prayer in the Garden was not to avoid bearing our sins and dying for us, but to protect Him from Satan, who was there in the Garden about to take His life before He got to the cross. Hebrews 5:7 says, "Who in the days of his flesh, when he had offered up prayers and supplications with strong crying and tears unto him that was able to save him from death, and was heard in that he feared." Isn't that telling us God did hear and saved Him from dying in the Garden?

A. Well, you did ask a question, but you answered it yourself, and it may well be the correct answer. He did not want to miss the cross, but He didn't want to die in the Garden.

Q. Regarding Matthew 26:39, did Jesus know when He prayed, "O my Father, if it be possible, let this cup pass from me: nevertheless not as I will, but as thou wilt," that He would be forsaken?

A. Very frankly, I think our Lord understood that. You will recall in Matthew 20:20–28, when James and John wanted a place next to Him in His kingdom, one on the right side, one on the left, He asked them, "Are you able to drink of the cup that I shall drink of?" They thought they knew, so they said they could, but they didn't know.

They didn't know what was involved, but our Lord *did*. He took the cup of suffering, He drank that cup to the very dregs, because He knew exactly why He had come to the earth. He stated His mission again and again. And He told His disciples six months before He went to Jerusalem for the last time,

> Behold, we go up to Jerusalem; and the Son of man shall be betrayed unto the chief priests and unto the scribes, and they shall condemn him to death, and shall deliver him to the Gentiles to mock, and to scourge, and to crucify him: and the third day he shall rise again (Matt. 20:18–19).

He outlined the entire program for the final week, and He again stated His mission to the earth: "The Son of man came not to be ministered unto, but to minister, and to give his life a ransom for many" (Matt. 20:28).

TRIAL

Q. Is it true that the Jews are responsible for Christ's death?

A. A great many Christians get the wrong impression, thinking that because the nation officially rejected Jesus that the Jews rejected Him. May I say to you that when the nation rejected Him officially, He turned and dealt personally with the individual. No longer did He preach "the kingdom of heaven is at hand," the Messianic Kingdom which had been prophesied in the Old Testament and which He came to fulfill. Having been officially rejected, He turned to His own people and said literally, "Come unto me, all ye that labor and are heavy laden, and I will rest you," for He was a Savior, and He was the Savior for them.

Many Jews turned to Him. After His death upon the cross and His resurrection from the dead and His ascension back into heaven, *multitudes* of Jews believed in Christ. In the book of Acts we are told that even a multitude of *priests* turned to Christ! Sometimes we forget that the early church was 100 percent Jewish! And in Jerusalem, until about A.D. 100, no one but Jews were in the church. My friend, had you and I as Gentiles been in Jerusalem in the days of the apostle Paul, I don't think that either of us could have joined that church. We never would have gotten in because we were Gentiles. The early church was 100 percent Jewish. All the apostles were Jews. The New Testament, as well as the Old Testament, was written by Jewish writers.

Through the centuries there has been a remnant of Jewish believers "according to grace." God said that never, never in the history of the Hebrew race would there come a time when there would not be a remnant of them that were obedient to Him. And there is a remnant today. Always there has been a believing remnant of these people.

Q. What was the Roman responsibility for Christ's death?

A. First, let's look at the Roman governor Pilate and his place in the crucifixion of Jesus. When they brought Jesus to him, Pilate felt that the religious rulers had no basis for requesting the death penalty. Jesus had not incited rebellion against Rome. Others had, but Jesus had not. Pilate had a problem on his hands. He wanted to please the religious leaders in order to maintain peace in Jerusalem, but he felt that he could not arbitrarily sentence the Lord Jesus to death. So he hit upon a solution to the problem. Matthew tells us in chapter 27 that, since it was his habit to release a Jewish prisoner during the Passover celebration, he would offer the crowd a choice: Jesus or a very notorious prisoner called Barabbas, who was guilty of murder, robbery, treason—the whole bit. "Therefore when they were gathered together, Pilate said unto them, Whom will ye that I release unto you? Barabbas, or Jesus which is called Christ? For he knew that for envy they had delivered him" (vv. 17–18).

Pilate was a clever politician. He could see what was taking place, and he was sure that the crowd would ask for Barabbas to be crucified and Jesus to be released. This would give him a happy "out" to this situation.

But you see, the religious rulers were clever politicians themselves. They circulated among the crowd saying, "Ask that Barabbas be delivered and Jesus be destroyed." "The governor answered and said unto them, Whether of the twain will ye that I release unto you? They said, Barabbas" (v. 21).

Pilate was taken aback. He had not known how low religion would stoop. "Pilate saith unto them, What shall I do then with Jesus which is called Christ? They all say unto him, Let him be crucified" (v. 22). Imagine a Roman judge asking a crowd what he should do with a prisoner! Pilate was the judge, and he should make the decision. The Gospel of John tells us that Pilate repeatedly called Jesus inside the judgment hall and questioned Him privately. His thought seemed to be, "Jesus, if You will cooperate with me, I can get You out of this, and it will get me off this hot seat I'm on!" But the Lord Jesus would not defend Himself. When we analyze this mock trial, we come to the conclusion that Pilate was the one on trial and, actually, that Jesus was the Judge. "When Pilate saw that he could prevail nothing, but that rather a tumult was made, he took water, and washed his hands before the multitude, saying, I am innocent of the blood of this just person: see ye to it" (v. 24).

But it was not that easy. Pilate had to make a decision—every man does. It was John Newton who wrote:

> "What think ye of Christ?" is the test,
>> To try both your state and your scheme;
> You cannot be right in the rest,
>> Unless you think rightly of Him.

Although Pilate washed his hands, the bitter irony of it is that in the oldest creed of the church stand these words: "crucified under Pontius Pilate." The blood of Jesus was on his hands no matter how much he washed them. "Then answered all the people, and said, His blood be on us, and on our children" (v. 25).

Horrible as it has been, that has been the case, and it can be so demonstrated.

CRUCIFIXION

Q. Did Jesus remain on the cross overnight?

A. He did not. It was the time of the feast, and that would not have been permitted.

The Jews therefore, because it was the preparation, that the bodies should not remain upon the cross on the sabbath day, (for that sabbath day was an high day,) besought Pilate that their legs might be broken, and that they might be taken away (John 19:31).

Q. When Christ was crucified, why did He say, "My God, my God," instead of "My Father, my Father, why hast thou forsaken me" (Matt. 27:46)?

A. Well, if you will recall, Jesus was made sin for us—He who knew no sin—so that God must separate Himself from Him. As a result, God the Father and God the Son were divided at that moment when the Son was made sin. I think it is highly appropriate that He should have said, "My God," and not "My Father," at a time like that, because sin puts us all in the position of not being sons of God. You and I are not sons of God until we have come to Christ and have received Him as Savior.

Now a savior is a savior from something. What is Jesus the Savior from? He is the Savior from sin. He is the Savior from the *penalty* of sin by His death about 2,000 years ago, and He can save us today from the *power* of sin by the Holy Spirit. He is going to save us someday from the *presence* of sin, for He is going to take us to a place where there is no sin. And if He gets us there, the sin question is sure going to have to be settled in our hearts and in our lives at that time because no sin is going to enter into that city. "And there shall in no wise enter into it any thing that defileth, neither whatsoever worketh abomination, or maketh a lie: but they which are written in the Lamb's book of life" (Rev. 21:27).

Q. You declared that Christ's cross was probably one upright piece of wood. How in the world could anyone make a cross from one upright chunk of a tree?

A. There are two or three things which I would like to clear up. One regards the King James Version. You say I consider it the very Word of God. Actually I consider it the best translation we have from the Word of God, but you need to recognize that it is a *translation*. There are places where a better word could be substituted to help in our understanding of the Greek or Hebrew word being used.

Now about the shape of the cross. I agree with you that if you're going to translate the word used as *cross* you've got to have one piece of wood put across another. But actually the Greek word *stauros*, which is translated "cross," could mean a walking stick or a piece of plank—just one piece. That's one reason I think the Lord was crucified on just one upright.

We need to realize that the Roman government was not making a lot of pretty crosses to crucify men on in that day; they wouldn't have taken the time to do that. Their way of doing it would have been very rough and crude and cruel.

Q. If Jesus had brothers and sisters, why did our Lord request on the cross that the apostle John take care of His mother Mary? Why couldn't the brothers and sisters take care of her?

A. Let me suggest several things to you. I don't think Jesus' brothers were converted until after the Resurrection. They were obviously converted then, but up to that time they were not on good terms with Him. And they were probably not too loyal to their mother. The Lord Jesus knew He could depend on John. And John apparently was rather well-to-do, at least upper middle-class, as we would say today. This man was able to take care of her, and the Lord Jesus didn't want her put in a retirement home. He told John to treat her as his own mother.

Now somebody's going to write and say, "Well, there were no retirement places in that day." Yes, there were. But the places where the poor were kept were horrible! Our Lord Jesus wanted to spare her. His mother was there at the cross, loyal to Him to the very end. But the brothers and sisters apparently were not; they are not mentioned. Therefore I think that we have a very reasonable explanation of why He asked John to take care of her. The amazing thing is that while He was there dying in agony, He was thinking of someone taking care of His mother. This is one of the loveliest gestures of His humanity when He was here on this earth.

DEATH

Q. Recently I heard that when Jesus went to hell to set the captives free, He suffered the torments of hell to complete our redemption. Do you know a Scripture that would support or refute this teaching?

A. Well, I don't think you need Scripture to refute it. You need Scripture that teaches it. I'm of the opinion that the Scripture you may have in mind is 1 Peter 3:18–19: "For Christ also hath once suffered for sins, the just for the unjust, that he might bring us to God, being put to death in the flesh, but quickened by the Spirit: by which also he went and preached unto the spirits in prison."

The question is, when did Christ speak by the Spirit to those who were then in prison? Was it at the time they were in prison? No, it goes on to say in verse 20: "Which sometime were disobedient, when once the longsuffering of God waited in the days of Noah, while the ark was a-preparing, wherein few, that is, eight souls were saved by water."

Now the interesting thing here is that the time that the Spirit of God preached to these people was in the days of Noah, and through Noah God preached to them. In other words, those who were judged in the Flood heard the preaching of Noah. Now at the time Peter writes this, those who were judged in the Flood were the spirits in prison, waiting for the judgment. But to say that Christ went down and made that announcement to them or preached to them is just not quite the thought here. And it is certainly not the language of the apostle Peter, by any means.

RESURRECTION

Q. Someone who came to my door said that Jesus didn't resurrect bodily but only as a spirit. What does the Bible say?

A. The Bible has a great deal to say about the resurrection of Jesus Christ. The arch of the gospel rests upon two great pillars: the death of Christ and the resurrection of Christ. Listen to the apostle Paul as he defines the gospel: "For I delivered unto you first of all that which I also received, how that Christ died for our sins according to the scriptures; and that he was buried, and that he rose again the third day according to the scriptures" (1 Cor. 15:3–4).

Regarding the order of events connected with the resurrection of Christ, I would like to share with you a very fine note found in the *The Scofield Reference Bible* on page 1043:

> The order of events, combining the four narratives, is as follows: Three women, Mary Magdalene, and Mary the mother of James, and Salome, start for the sepulchre, followed by other women bearing spices. The three find the stone rolled away, and Mary Magdalene goes to tell the disciples (Luke 23:55—24:9; John 20:1, 2). Mary, the mother of James and Joses, draws nearer the tomb and sees the angel of the Lord (Matt. 28:2). She goes back to meet the other women following with the spices. Meanwhile Peter and John, warned by Mary Magdalene, arrive, look in, and go away (John 20:3–10). Mary Magdalene returns weeping, sees the two angels and then Jesus (John 20:11–18), and goes as He bade her to tell the disciples. Mary (mother of James and Joses), meanwhile, has met the women with the spices and, returning with them, they see the two angels (Luke 24:4, 5; Mark 16:5). They also receive the angelic message, and, going to seek the disciples, are met by Jesus (Matt. 28:8–10).
>
> The order of our Lord's appearances would seem to be: On the day of His resurrection: (1) To Mary Magdalene (John 20:14–18). (2) To the women returning from the tomb with the angelic message (Matt. 28:8–10). (3) To Peter, probably in the afternoon (Luke 24:34; 1 Cor. 15:5). (4) To the Emmaus disciples toward evening (Luke 24:13–31). (5) To the apostles, except Thomas (Luke 24:36–43; John 20:19–24). Eight days afterward:

(1) To the apostles, Thomas being present (John 20:24–29). In Galilee: (1) To the seven by the Lake of Tiberias (John 21:1–23). (2) On a mountain, to the apostles and five hundred brethren (1 Cor. 15:6). At Jerusalem and Bethany again: (1) To James (1 Cor. 15:7). (2) To the eleven (Mark 16:14–20; Luke 24:33–53; Acts 1:3–12). To Paul: (1) Near Damascus (Acts 9:3–6; 1 Cor. 15:8). (2) In the temple (Acts 22:17–21; 23:11). To Stephen, outside Jerusalem (Acts 7:55). To John on Patmos (Rev. 1:10–19).

The liberal church and several cults use 1 Corinthians 15:44 to sustain the theory that the resurrection is spiritual. Let us see if the passage remotely suggests a spiritual resurrection: "It is sown a natural body; it is raised a spiritual body. There is a natural body, and there is a spiritual body."

On the contrary, this verse is the undoing of the false hypothesis that the resurrection is only spiritual. A careful consideration of certain words will reveal this. The words *natural* and *spiritual* are adjectives; *body* is the noun and appears twice. Now, a noun is stronger than an adjective. Therefore, the body is implicated in resurrection. The body is sown one kind and raised another; nevertheless, it is still a body. The present body is a physiological (natural) body. The new body which will be raised will be pneumatical (spiritual). Although at the resurrection the new body will be motivated and will function differently from the present body, the fact remains that it is a *body*. The resurrection *always* refers to the body.

Q. I would like to know where in the Bible it says that Christ arose on Easter Sunday. I have found only the following:

- Matthew 28:1: "In the end of the sabbath, as it began to dawn toward the first day of the week . . ."
- Mark 16:1: "And when the sabbath was past . . ."

- Luke 24:1–2: "Now upon the first day of the week, very early in the morning . . . they found the stone rolled away from the sepulchre."

- John 20:1: "The first day of the week . . . when it was yet dark . . ."

A. The first day of the week is Sunday according to our calendar today. It is true that the word *Sunday* is not used in the Scripture and it is true that the calendar shifted around and the names of the days of the week came in later. But the basic fact is that Christ arose from the dead at Passover time, which is determined by the new moon and the first day of the week. Now if you don't want to call it Sunday, you call it whatever you want to call it.

As for the word *Easter,* it is used only once in the Scriptures, in the book of Acts;

> *Now about that time Herod the king stretched forth his hands to vex certain of the church . . . and because he saw it pleased the Jews he proceeded further to take Peter also. (Then were the days of unleavened bread. And when he had apprehended him, he put him in prison, and delivered him to four quaternions of soldiers to keep him; intending after Easter to bring him forth to the people (Acts 12:1–4).*

I don't think that your question is really pertinent because it is now an established historic fact that Jesus died, He was buried, He rose again. Why waste your time arguing about those other details? Today we need so much to get out the Word of God that when we stop and debate these minor issues, it seems to me a great waste of time.

Q. Why did Christ tell Mary not to touch Him before He ascended?

A. Let's read John 20:17: "Jesus saith unto her [Mary Magdalene], Touch me not; for I am not yet ascended to my Father: but go to my brethren, and say unto them, I ascend unto my Father, and your Father; and to my God, and your God."

First of all, the word *touch* is *haptomai* "to hold on to." Jesus Christ at that time was the great High Priest. At His encounter with Mary He was on the way to present His sacrifice in the Holy of Holies—in heaven itself, as the writer to the Hebrews said. I take the position that Jesus presented His literal blood in heaven and that He was on His way there. But He said to Mary, "You go and tell my brethren." Then if you will notice, He said, "I ascend to my Father and to your Father." You see, the relationship in the Trinity of Father and Son is a different kind of relationship because the Son is not generated. God is the eternal Father of the eternal Son, the Lord Jesus Christ. God becomes our Father when we trust the Lord Jesus as our Savior. At that time we are born again into the family of God, and He becomes our Father. That is a distinction that Jesus very definitely is making in this passage of Scripture.

Now let's move on down. Having presented His sacrifice, He appears then to His disciples. At that time, according to Luke 24:39, He said to them in effect, "Handle Me, and make sure that I am real, that this is not a spirit you are seeing." And He even ate fish there to demonstrate that He was flesh and bone. Note that it says flesh and bone, not flesh and blood, because He had presented His blood. He was living in a glorified body in which, apparently, life comes from something other than the blood.

The kind of body that you and I have is a body that is made alive because of the blood. God said, "The life of the flesh is in the blood: and I have given it to you. . . to make an atonement for your souls" (Lev. 17:11). Blood was given as the sacrifice, you see.

GLORIFICATION

Q. When was Jesus glorified? When Judas left the Upper Room, Jesus said He was now glorified. I've always been taught that Jesus was not glorified until after He went to heaven, but John 13:31 seems to refute that. Please explain.

A. Well, if John 13:31 is telling you that Jesus was glorified before He went to heaven, then it contradicts another passage of Scripture just a few chapters over. And I'll be honest with you, I think John the apostle had sense enough to not put in a contradiction. So maybe the contradiction is in our thinking today and not in John's Gospel.

Let's look at John 13:31: "Therefore, when he was gone out, Jesus said, Now is the Son of man glorified, and God is glorified in him."

How is God glorified in Him? Remember that Jesus is moving toward the cross. Judas is going to betray Him, to sell Him. Jesus is going to the Garden of Gethsemane. He is to be arrested. He will go through the agony of the Garden, and then He will go to trial and then to the cross. And God was glorified in that, for that is what Jesus came to do—the Father's will. But that is not the glory of Deity, that is not the glory of Christ, because in the Lord's prayer in John 17 He says, "I have glorified thee on the earth: I have finished the work which thou gavest me to do" (v. 4).

He says to the Father, "I have glorified You." That was what He was talking about in chapter 13:31.

And again Jesus says, "And now, O Father, glorify thou me with thine own self with the glory which I had with thee before the world was" (John 17:5). Now that glory which He had as God He had laid aside—not His deity, but all that went with it, all the accoutrements of glory, all that should have come to Him. And He came to this earth, just a carpenter, and went to the cross. But now He is coming back to the Father and is saying, "Glorify me with that glory."

SECOND COMING

Q. Is Christ with us now or is He coming at some future time?

A. He is coming at a future time. I think we need to bring in a little logic and put the Scripture in order. He said to His disciples, preparing them for the time He would go back to heaven, "Nevertheless I tell you the truth; It is expedient for you that I go away: for if I go not away, the Comforter will not come unto you; but if I depart, I will send him unto you" (John 16:7). The Holy Spirit takes the things of Christ and makes them real to us. So the Holy Spirit, the Spirit of Christ, is here, and Christ is there at the right hand of the Father.

Q. I have assumed that when Jesus said He was going away temporarily He was referring to the Resurrection. And His return will be the Second Coming. What do you think?

A. Well, His going away was not the Resurrection. His going away was His ascension into heaven. The Second Coming is, strictly speaking, His return to the earth to set up His kingdom. But He's coming first to take believers (collectively referred to as the church) out of the world. The common name for this phase of His coming is the Rapture, which we believe will be before the Great Tribulation period.

I think He has made it clear we are not going to blow up the planet. And the reason I say this is because the Lord Jesus Christ in the Olivet Discourse (Matt. 24) says that there will be a restraint over evil and that men will not be able to go as far as they would like to go. That is true today. The Holy Spirit keeps the human family from being meaner than it is. That may seem unbelievable, because it is very mean now, but I think there is that restraint.

Then you make the statement that His return may be millions of years hence. Now any logical interpretation would be that we cannot know the date, but we can say that it would not be millions of years away because it is estimated man has been on this earth only about 5,000 years. The Scripture makes it clear that Christ is coming back to pick up His church before the Great Tribulation period. Therefore I don't believe it could be millions of years; your logic is unreasonable when you consider the way God in the past has dealt with mankind. A thousand or two, or maybe three thousand years is the length of any of the dispensations of the past. It doesn't seem possible we could have a million years ahead of us!

SECTION THREE

DOCTRINE

ANGELS

Q. Why did God create angels? What is their function? Do we have guardian angels?

A. The word *angel* (*aggelos*) means messenger and may be applied to a human or divine messenger. According to Scripture there is an order of supernatural creatures. I think it would really surprise us if we had any concept of the number of angels in the universe. They are called the host of heaven, and that means there are a whole lot of them. Their numbers apparently are not diminished or added to in any way, but we have no idea how many angels there are. They have an important part in God's plan.

Angels were prominent in their ministry to Israel in the Old Testament. The Law was given by the agency of angels (Ps. 68:17; Acts 7:53; Gal. 3:19). Cherubim were woven into the veil of the tabernacle and fashioned of gold for the mercy seat. Isaiah had a vision of the seraphim. And according to the book of Revelation, after the church is removed an angelic ministry of judgment takes place.

The angels of God are wonderful, but they are, of course, inferior to the Son. They are *His* angels, *His* ministers, and *His* worshipers. "And of the angels he saith, Who maketh his angels spirits, and his ministers a flame of fire" (Heb. 1:7). This is a quotation from Psalm 104:4. The angels belong to the Lord.

My feeling is that the angelic ministry is not connected with the church at all. This subject is becoming exceedingly difficult and dangerous today because there is a manifestation of demonism. Several writers are saying that demons are directing them, but they call them angels. My friend, an angelic ministry is not for our day.

But someone is going to say to me, "But we have a guardian angel." Where did that idea come from? I don't think we have guardian angels. Some people say, "Oh, but we each need to have a guardian angel." Let me ask you a question: Are you a child of God? If you are, you are indwelt by the Holy Spirit of God, who is the third person of the Godhead. What could a guardian angel do for you that the Holy Spirit can't do for you? Do you want to think that over for a while?

The idea of an active angelic ministry in the church came about because some of the early church members who were marvelous artists liked to paint angels.

If you have ever been in the Sistine Chapel in Rome and looked up at the ceiling, you probably felt that angels were hovering over you. They are as thick as pigeons up there. Michelangelo certainly did like to paint angels. Although I am glad that I've seen the Sistine Chapel, I wouldn't give five cents to see it again because it teaches that there are angels connected with our lives today. My friend *we* have to do with a *living Savior!* Let's just push the angels aside because we don't have to go to God through angels. We have the Holy Spirit, and we have Christ, our great intercessor. Let us get our minds off of angels and center them upon the person of Christ. He is superior to angels.

BAPTISM

Q. Must I be baptized to be saved? Why do some churches consider baptism by immersion to be so important?

A. First of all, I want to say that I do not deal with questions on the mode of baptism because I do not believe that baptism is essential to salvation. After you're saved then there may be room for a discussion about the mode of baptism. There is a sharp division in good churches today over that mode, and I refuse to get into that argument simply because it is not part of the gospel. Paul wrote to the Corinthians to define the gospel, and, friend, you just can't find a drop of water in the gospel there.

> Moreover, brethren, I declare unto you the gospel which I preached unto you, which also ye have received, and wherein ye stand; by which also ye are saved, if ye keep in memory what I preached unto you, unless ye have believed in vain. For I delivered unto you first of all that which I also received, how that Christ died for our sins according to the scriptures; and that he was buried, and that he rose again the third day according to the scriptures (1 Cor. 15:1–4).

Now those two basic facts, the death of Christ and the resurrection of Christ, are essential for our salvation. He "was delivered for our offences, and was raised again for our justification" (Rom. 4:25). Now that is the gospel, and I want to confine my teaching to that issue and that issue alone.

I'm a graduate of a Presbyterian seminary, a Presbyterian college, and a Presbyterian prep school, and if anybody was ever indoctrinated about sprinkling, I sure was. But in my ministry I have come to the position that immersion sets forth the thing our Lord did for us: that we are buried with Him in identification, He died for us; we are raised with Him in newness of life and that is what saves us. Baptism represents it, therefore baptism is *believer's* baptism. You do not get baptized to get saved, you get baptized because you *are* saved.

Q. You say water baptism is not necessary for our salvation. How do you explain 1 Peter 3:21?

A. Let's look at that for a moment: "The like figure whereunto even baptism doth also now save us (not the putting away of the filth of the flesh, but the answer of a good conscience toward God) by the resurrection of Jesus Christ" (1 Pet. 3:21).

To what baptism does this refer? This is not water baptism but the baptism of the Holy Spirit. The baptism of the Holy Spirit is *real* baptism, and water baptism is *ritual* baptism. Now I believe in water baptism, and I believe immersion is the proper mode. However, the important thing here is that it is the baptism of the Holy Spirit which puts you into the body of believers.

"Not the putting away of the filth of the flesh": it is not just by water, for that will not put away the filth of the flesh. "But the answer of a good conscience toward God, by the resurrection of Jesus Christ": that is, a faith in the resurrection of Jesus Christ which brought the work of the Holy Spirit into your life and regenerated you.

"Who is gone into heaven, and is on the right hand of God; angels and authorities and powers being made subject unto him" (1 Pet. 3:22). This verse is speaking of the Lord Jesus Christ. You and I are little sinners down here, but we can come to Him, receive Him, and thus join the great company of the redeemed. We are baptized by the Holy Spirit into the body of Christ because He is raised from the dead and is today at God's right hand.

One can get to heaven without being baptized, like the thief on the cross. More than 200 times in the New Testament salvation is said to be conditioned solely on the basis of faith. You and I are saved by being identified with Christ.

He identified Himself with us in baptism. And Peter says that we are saved by baptism. In what way? By being identified with the Lord Jesus. To be saved is to be in Christ. How do we get into Christ? By the baptism of the Holy Spirit. I believe in water baptism because by it we declare that we are identified with Christ. The Lord Jesus said, "Him that cometh to me I will in no wise cast out" (John 6:37). We must recognize that we have to be identified with Christ, and that is accomplished by the Holy Spirit. Our water baptism is a testimony.

One time an old salt said to a sailor in trying to get the young man to accept Christ and be baptized, "Young man, it is *duty* or *mutiny!*" And when you come to Christ, my friend, you are to be baptized because it is a duty. If you do not, it is mutiny.

This subject of baptism needs to be lifted out of the realm of argument to the high and lofty plane of standing for Christ. How we need to come out and stand for Christ!

Q. Where does it say, "One faith, one Lord, one baptism"? I understand this verse to refer to one's being born again and joined to the body of Christ, not water baptism.

A. Probably we ought to turn to Ephesians 4:4–6: "There is one body, and one Spirit, even as ye are called in one hope of your calling; one Lord, one faith, one baptism, one God and Father of all, who is above all, and through all, and in you all."

Well, I personally believe with you that it is not water (ritual) baptism in this verse but actually the real baptism, which is the baptism of the Holy Spirit. But I *do* think that ritual baptism should be performed in order to show that the baptism of the Spirit has taken place.

- "One body"—is the total number of believers from Pentecost to the Rapture.

- "One Spirit"—refers to the Holy Spirit who baptizes each believer into the body of Christ.

- "One hope of your calling"—refers to the goal set before all believers.

- "One Lord"—is the Lord Jesus Christ. His lordship over believers brings into existence the unity of the church.

- "One faith"—is faith in the plenary, verbal inspiration of the Scriptures, in the deity of Christ, and in redemption—the substitutionary death of Christ upon the cross, the vicarious death of Christ for your sins and mine.

- "One baptism"—refers to the baptism of the Holy Spirit. "For by one Spirit are we all baptized into one body . . ." (1 Cor. 12:13). Paul is talking here about one body and he's talking about one Lord and one faith and one Spirit. So he has to be referring to the baptism of the Holy Spirit that puts us into the body of believers.

BIBLE

Q. Is every word of the Bible true?

A. I cover this in my answer regarding the inspiration of Scripture, but the word *inerrancy* is being kicked around these days, so let me start with a definition. Inerrancy has to do with the principle of freedom from error. This is not a specific doctrine of Scripture.

Dr. Lewis Sperry Chafer has excellent definitions, and I can't improve on his definition of inerrancy. Let me quote some excerpts:

The Bible is not such a book as man would write if he could, or could write if he would. Devout men, some of great scholarship, have always agreed in the main as to the inerrant and supernatural qualities of the Bible. It must be conceded that God is able to produce a book which is verbally accurate.

Granting that God has a body of truth which he would enjoin upon man, it is not difficult to recognize the importance of an inerrant record of that body of truth. Nor is it a matter of surprise that an increasing pressure is exerted, first from one group and then another, to break down the Bible's own testimony regarding its inspiration. That doctrine of inspiration which the church has held in all her generations, abides, not because its defenders are able to shout louder than their opponents, nor by the virtue of any human defense, but because of the fact that it is embedded within the divine oracles themselves. The Spirit of God has declared, "Every word of God is pure" (Prov. 30:5).

Q. Our pastor preaches strong gospel on Sunday. But in his Bible study he tells us that the story of creation is not the story of the creation of the world but rather a story of the creation of the Jewish race; that there were people living in China long before the time Adam and Eve were brought into existence; that Moses never wrote the first five books of the Bible and that there was no writing before the time of Ezra; that following the Revolutionary War all the Christians that were left in the United States were Methodists; and that the World Council of Churches will bring about the return of the Lord.

A. Heresy—I've never heard so much heresy in so small a compass as you are getting in this particular area. The young man who is your pastor is the product of modern denominational seminaries. He is apparently neo-orthodox. He can at one time preach the gospel and then at another time can deny everything that is said in the Bible except the gospel. But how can you believe one and reject the other?

This theory is a very old story. Genesis is not dated and gives no date for the creation of Adam and Eve. For him to categorically say there were people in China before then, when we don't know the time of *then,* is merely a figment of the imagination. That is the old Graf-Wellhausen hypothesis, the old German theory that brought Germany under Hitler. Having rejected the Bible and Jesus Christ, they naturally were prepared to accept Hitler. That theory is discredited today, except by those who haven't anything else to hold onto. So that we can just say this is a new twist to an old theory, and it has no value whatsoever. It's not even scholarly to hold theories that have no more basis than that.

Now when he says Moses did not write the first five books of the Bible, that again is the old Graf-Wellhausen hypothesis—it's long been exploded by conservative scholars and it's pretty well established today that Moses did write the Pentateuch. Your young pastor has been given only one theory and a very dangerous theory at that.

Q. What does it mean to say the Bible has been *inspired?*

A. I personally believe in what is known as the plenary verbal inspiration of the Scriptures, which means that the Bible is an authoritative statement and that every word of it is the Word of God to us and for us in this day in which we live. Inspiration guarantees the revelation of God, and that is exactly what this Book says. Two men, Paul writing his last epistle to Timothy and Peter writing his last epistle, both had something definite to say about the Bible.

"All scripture is given by inspiration of God, and is profitable for doctrine, for reproof, for correction, for instruction in righteousness: that the man of God may be perfect, thoroughly furnished unto all good works" (2 Tim. 3:16–17). Notice *all* Scripture is given by inspiration. The word *inspiration* means *God breathed.* God said through these men, as He said here through Paul, exactly what He wanted to say. He hasn't anything else to add. Peter expresses it this way: "For the prophecy came not in old time by the will of man; but holy men of God spake as they were moved by the Holy Ghost" (2 Pet. 1:21).

It is very important to see that these men were moved, or carried along by the Holy Spirit of God. Bishop Westcott said: "The thoughts are wedded to words as necessarily as the soul is to the body." And Dr. Keiper said, "You can as easily have music without notes, or mathematics without figures, as thoughts without words." The *thoughts* are not inspired; the *words* are inspired.

There is a whimsical story of a girl who had taken singing lessons from a very famous teacher. He was present at her recital, and after it was over she was anxious to know his reaction. He didn't come back to congratulate her, and she asked a friend, "What did he say?" Her loyal friend answered, "He said that you sang heavenly." She couldn't quite believe that her teacher had said that, so she probed, "Is that *exactly* what he said?" "Well, no, but that is what he meant." The girl insisted, "Tell me the exact *words* he used." "Well, his exact words were, 'That was an unearthly noise!'" May I say to you, there is a difference between unearthly noise and heavenly sound. Exact words are important.

Believe me, it is the words of Scripture that are inspired—not the thought, but the words. For instance, Satan was not inspired to tell a lie, but the Bible records that he told a lie. The Lord Jesus said, "It is written," quoting the Word of God in the Old Testament—the men who wrote gave out what God had to say. In Exodus 20:1 Moses wrote: "And God spake all these words, saying . . ." God did the speaking; Moses wrote what He said.

Over the years many excellent manuscripts of the Scriptures have been discovered. Speaking of the manuscripts in Britain, Sir George Kenyon, the late director and principal librarian of the British Museum, made this statement: "Thanks to these manuscripts, the ordinary reader of the Bible may feel comfortable about the soundness of the text. Apart from a few unimportant verbal alterations, natural in books transcribed by hand, the New Testament, we now feel assured, has come down intact." We can be sure today that we have that which is as close to the autographs as anything possibly can be, and I believe in the verbal plenary inspiration of the autographs—that is, the original manuscripts.

Q. Why does the Roman Catholic Bible have more books than the Protestant Bible?

A. The Roman Catholic Bible includes the Apocrypha which was written after the end of the Old Testament and before the beginning of the New Testament. This intertestamental period of 400 years was a time of great literary activity in spite of the fact there was no revelation from God. The Old Testament was translated into Greek in Alexandria, Egypt, during the period from 285 to 247 B.C. and was called the *Septuagint*. This translation was used by Paul, and our Lord apparently quoted from it.

The fourteen books of the Old Testament Apocrypha were written during this era and bear no marks of inspiration. There are two books classified as the pseudepigrapha: the *Psalter of Solomon* and the *Book of Enoch*. Although they bear the names of two men described in the Old Testament, there is no evidence that these men were the writers.

In some Protestant Bibles the Apocrypha is inserted in a separate block of literature between Old and New Testaments because the books shed some light on the 400-year lapse between the testaments. However, they are not regarded as part of the inspired Word of God for many reasons, one of which is that our Lord Jesus never referred to them or quoted from them as He did the thirty-nine books of the Old Testament.

BOOK OF LIFE

Q. Can one's name be blotted out from the book of life, as Revelation 3:5 seems to suggest?

A. Here is the verse in question: "He that overcometh, the same shall be clothed in white raiment; and I will not blot out his name out of the book of life, but I will confess his name before my Father, and before his angels" (Rev. 3:5).

If you understand this to mean that a believer can lose his salvation, my answer is no. If you are a true believer in Christ, your name can never be blotted out in the sense that you would lose your salvation.

If you are trusting Him, then you can be sure of one thing: He is able to save you and keep you saved. That is *His* work, by the way, not yours.

Actually, the statement, "I will not blot out his name out of the book of life," is very difficult to understand. I am confident that none of us has a complete, adequate, and full interpretation.

First of all, what is this book of life? Many commentators spiritualize this book away. I have no intention of doing that because I find mention of this book of life all the way through the Word of God.

Moses evidently referred to this book in Exodus 32:32 as he interceded for his people. "Yet now, if thou wilt forgive their sin—;and if not, blot me, I pray thee, out of thy book which thou hast written." Moses' name was in the book, and he was actually asking God to blot his name out—which I think would not have been possible—but nevertheless he was willing to go that far.

Also, you will find that the psalmist over in Psalm 69:28 refers to the blotting out of names. "Let them be blotted out of the book of the living, and not be written with the righteous."

And Daniel 12:1 is a very familiar verse:

And at that time shall Michael stand up, the great prince which standeth for the children of thy people: and there shall be a time of trouble, such as never was since there was a nation even to that same time: and at that time thy people shall be delivered, every one that shall be found written in the book.

Again, this is a reference to names written in a book. Notice that in all of these Old Testament references there is the concept of a name that has been entered and then the possibility of a name being removed.

Now, we want to go to the New Testament and let our Lord speak, for He has something to say about it: "Notwithstanding in this rejoice not, that the spirits are subject unto you; but rather rejoice, because your names are written in heaven" (Luke 10:20). You'll find that Paul mentions this over in Philippians 4:3: "And I intreat thee also, true yokefellow, help those women which laboured with me in the gospel, with Clement also, and with other my fellowlabourers, whose names are in the book of life."

We see a constant reference through the Bible to this book; and that, by the way, doesn't exhaust all of the passages where it occurs. Consider Hebrews 12:23: "To the general assembly and church of the firstborn, which are written in heaven, and to God the Judge of all, and to the spirits of just men made perfect."

In the book of Revelation, although Revelation 3:5 is the first reference, it is certainly not the last reference to the book of life. In Revelation 13:8, for instance: "And all that dwell upon the earth shall worship him, whose names are not written in the book of life of the Lamb slain from the foundation of the world." Also, Revelation 17:8:

The beast that thou sawest was, and is not; and shall ascend out of the bottomless pit, and go into perdition: and they that dwell on the earth shall wonder, whose names were not written in the book of life from the foundation of the world, when they behold the beast that was, and is not, and yet is.

When you come to the Great White Throne of Judgment this book is brought out, and the ones who are judged are those whose names are not in the book of life.

And I saw the dead, small and great, stand before God; and the books were opened: and another book was opened, which is the book of life: and the dead were judged out of those things which were written in the books, according to their works (Rev. 20:12).

The book of life was there and the test was whether the name was in it. "And whosoever was not found written in the book of life was cast into the lake of fire" (Rev. 20:15). There have been quite a few interpretations of this, but let me present what I believe. There are evidently two books. In Genesis 5:1 we are told of "the book of the generations of Adam," and then in the New Testament in Matthew 1:1, "The book of the generation of Jesus Christ," and that book includes all the family.

All of us are in the book of Adam—"in Adam all die" (1 Cor. 15:22). That is the book of death. There is also a book of life, and that book is the book of the family of Jesus Christ. Now let me put it like this: I think that at birth every person's name is put in that book, because Jesus died for all. He is not only the propitiation for our sins, but for the sins of the *whole world*. When any of us comes to the end of life without having accepted Jesus Christ, then that person's name is removed from the book of life. But up to that time, we have ample opportunity to accept the Lord Jesus Christ as Savior and ample opportunity to make a decision. As long as we are alive down here that book is kept open, but there comes a time when it is too late.

This is exactly what our Lord is saying here to the church of Sardis in Revelation 3:4–5:

Thou hast a few names even in Sardis which have not defiled their garments; and they shall walk with me in white: for they are worthy. He that overcometh, the same shall be clothed in white raiment; and I will not blot out his name out of the book of life, but I will confess his name before my Father, and before his angels.

Our churches are filled with a great many people who are not saved. I'm sure you agree with me. Are they in the Lamb's Book of Life? I think so. But their names are not going to stay there unless they make a decision for Christ. Our Lord says to this church of Sardis, "I'll not blot out his name out of the book of life, but I'll confess his name before my Father, and before his angels." You see, when that man confesses Christ, then our Lord confesses him, and the name is kept in the book of life.

Certainly I do not believe this means you can be saved one day and you can be lost the next. There's not an eraser on God's pencil.

Q. My pastor says the Genesis account of creation was never meant to be taken literally and that any thinking person knows that evolution is true. What do you think?

A. This problem of origin provokes more violent controversy, wild theories, and wide disagreement than any other. Always there is the inclusion of men's hypotheses, and as a result there is a babble of voices that has drowned out the clear voice of God. Actually, there are two extreme groups who have blurred the issue. They have muddied the waters of understanding by their dogmatic assumptions and assertions. One group is comprised of the arrogant scientists who assume that biological and philosophical evolution are the gospel truth. Their assumed axiom is "the assured finding of science." The other group is comprised of the young and proud theologians who arrogate to themselves the superknowledge that they have discovered how God did it. They write and speak learnedly about some clever theory that reconciles science and the Bible.

I would say that both of these groups would do well to consider the question asked Job when the Lord finally appeared to him. God asked: "Where wast thou when I laid the foundations of the earth? declare, if thou hast understanding" (Job 38:4). In other words, God is saying to man,

"You talk about the origin of the universe, but you don't even know where you were when I laid the foundation of the earth!" There are a great many theories about how the world began, but all of them can be boiled down to fit into a two-fold classification: one is creation and the other is speculation. All theories fall into one of these two divisions.

Many different theories comprise the theory of evolution in our day. Some of the most reputable scientists of the past, as well as of the present, reject evolution. So we can't put down the theory of evolution as being a scientific statement like $2 + 2 = 4$. Then there is the creation account in Genesis 1, which must be accepted by faith. It is very interesting that God has made it that way. Notice what the writer to the Hebrews said: "Now faith is the substance of things hoped for, the evidence of things not seen. For by it the elders obtained a good report. Through faith we understand that the worlds were framed by the word of God, so that things which are seen were not made of things which do appear" (Heb. 11:1–3). So today the great problem still remains: how did the world get from nothing to something? The only way that you can ever arrive at an answer is by faith or by speculation—and speculation is not scientific.

Now look at some of the theories of origin. There are those who tell us that we should accept the scientific answer. I would like to ask, what is the scientific answer? What science are we talking about? In the year 1806 Professor Lyell said that the French Institute enumerated not less than eighty geological theories which were hostile to the Scriptures, but not one of these theories is held in our day.

Moses is the human agent whom God used to write the book of Genesis, and I think he would smile at all the disturbance today regarding the creation story because he did not write it with the intention of giving a scientific account. Paul tells us the purpose of all Scripture: "All scripture is given by inspiration of God, and is profitable for doctrine, for reproof, for correction, for instruction in righteousness: that the man of God may be perfect, thoroughly furnished unto all good works" (2 Tim. 3:16–17). The purpose of the

Scripture is for instruction in righteousness. It was not written to teach you geology or biology. It was written to show man's relationship to God and God's requirements for man and what man must do to be saved.

May I ask you, if God had given a scientific statement about creation, how many people of Moses' day could have understood it? How many people even in our day could grasp it? You must remember that the Bible was not written for learned professors only but also for simple folk of every age and in every land. If it had been written in the scientific language of Moses' time, it certainly would have been rejected.

Therefore, men have proposed several solutions relative to the origin of the universe. One is that it is an illusion. Well, that is certainly contrary to fact, is it not? And yet there are people who hold that theory. There are others who believe that it spontaneously arose out of nothing. (In a way, this is what the Bible states, although it goes further and says that God spoke it into existence; He created it.) Another view is that it had no origin but has existed eternally. A fourth view is that it was created, and this breaks down into many different theories which men hold in an attempt to explain the origin of the universe.

The evolutionary theory is divided up into many different phases and viewpoints and has never been demonstrated as being true. Unfortunately, when you get down to the level of the pseudoscientists—and I'm thinking of the teachers today in our public schools who teach science—they really are not in a position to give a fair view because they were given only one viewpoint in college.

I reject evolution because it rejects God and revelation, denies the fall of man and the fact of sin, and opposes the virgin birth of Christ. Therefore, I reject it with all my being. I do not believe that it is the answer to the origin of this universe.

There are three essential areas into which evolution cannot move and which evolution cannot solve. It cannot bridge the gap from nothing to something. It cannot bridge the gap from something to life. It cannot bridge the gap between life and humanity—that is, self-conscious human life with a free will.

Q. How long did it take God to create everything? Was it really in just six 24-hour days?

A. We see the construction of the universe in Genesis 1:1, the convulsion of the earth in verse 2, and then the construction of the earth in six days (vv. 3–31). I believe what we have here is this development.

There are several things that I would like to call to your attention. Exodus 20:11 reads, "For in six days the LORD made heaven and earth, the sea, and all that in them is." There is nothing in that verse about creating. It says "made"; God took that which was already formed and in those six days He did not "create," He re-created. He worked with matter which already existed. It was matter He had called into existence probably billions of years before.

The word *create* is from the Hebrew word *bara*, which means to create out of nothing. This word is used only three times in the first chapter of Genesis, because it records only three acts of creation. (1) The creation of something from nothing: "In the beginning God created the heaven and the earth" (1:1). (2) The creation of life: "And God created great whales, and every living creature that moveth" (v. 21). That's animal life of all kinds. (3) The creation of man: "So God created man in his own image" (v. 27).

God created life and put it on the earth, and for the earth He created man. That is the creature we are interested in because you and I happen to be one of those creatures. This makes the Genesis record intensely important for us today. Of the first day we read,

> And God said, Let there be light: and there was light. And God saw the light, that it was good: and God divided the light from the darkness. And God called the light Day, and the darkness he

*called Night. And the evening and the morning
were the first day* (Gen. 1:3–5).

That must have been a twenty-four hour day—I don't
see how you could get anything else out of it. Notice that
God said, "Let there be light." Ten times in this chapter we
will find "let there be"—let there be a firmament, let there
be lights, let the waters be gathered together, etc. Someone
has called these the ten commandments of creation.

Now let me say that theistic evolution is not the answer. It attempts to follow creation until the time of man,
then considers Adam and Eve to be products of some evolutionary process. The theistic evolutionist considers the days
in Genesis as periods of time, long periods of time. I do not
believe that is true. God's marking off the creative days with
the words, "And the evening and the morning were the first
day" etc., makes it clear that He was not referring to long
periods of time but to actual twenty-four hour days.

CREATION

Q. Did dinosaurs really exist? Why didn't Noah take
them on the ark?

A. What do we know about dinosaurs? I have heard this
whimsy about the guide in the museum who gave a
lecture to the crowd. When they came to the dinosaur he
said, "This dinosaur is two million and six years old." A
man came up to him and said, "Wait a minute. I'll accept
the two million years, but where do you get the six years?"
The guide answered, "Well, when I came to work here, that
dinosaur was two million years old. I've been here six years
now. So the dinosaur is now two million and six years old."

I ask again: what do we really know about dinosaurs?
You can ask any real scholar in any field and he will admit
that he is no authority—he hasn't mastered his field. He
will frankly say that he is just beginning to learn.

The media, of course, is always looking for something

sensational and comes up with interesting findings. Years ago a clipping was put into my hands from a fellow Texan about finding the tracks of dinosaurs near Glenrose, Texas, close to a place where I used to live. You might expect that in Texas they would find the biggest of everything, and apparently the dinosaurs were there. But later they found something quite disturbing: giant human tracks in the same place. I have noted that the media has ignored it because it is very difficult for evolutionists to start out with a little amoeba or a little scum on top of the water and then find that walking back there with the dinosaurs were human beings who were much bigger than any of us today.

Did Noah have a pair of dinosaurs on the ark? The Bible simply specifies that every living thing was to be included.

> *And of every living thing of all flesh, two of every sort shalt thou bring into the ark, to keep them alive with thee; they shall be male and female. Of fowls after their kind, and of cattle after their kind, of every creeping thing of the earth after his kind, two of every sort shall come unto thee, to keep them alive* (Gen. 6:19–20).

It is logical that at least all of the large animals were brought aboard as babies. If dinosaurs had not already died out, you may be sure that they were aboard.

CROSS

Q. Wasn't the thief on the cross saved without anything more than Christ at the moment?

A. Let's look at that thief for just a moment. All he said to the Lord Jesus was, "Remember me when You come into Your kingdom." That was nothing in the world but a simple act of faith. What are you going to tell that thief to do now? He has accepted Christ. Do you want to tell him to be baptized? He would say, "You're mocking me. Here I am nailed on a cross—I can't be baptized. I'm hanging up here." Suppose we say, "You ought to join the church." Well, there wasn't any church to join at that time because the day of Pentecost had not yet come. And suppose somebody else says, especially one of our good liberal preachers who go in for good works, "Well, brother, the thing you are to do is to run errands of mercy." He would say, "Wait a minute! My feet are nailed to this cross. I can't run errands of mercy." Then somebody else might say, "Well, you ought to do some good works." And he'd answer, "Look at my hands, they're nailed here. I can't do anything for anybody."

He couldn't do anything, friend, except trust the Lord Jesus. And that's all you and I can do because as far as good works are concerned and joining something and going through a ceremony—my friend, Paul said when he came to Jesus Christ that he flushed all that down:

> Yea doubtless, and I count all things but loss for the excellency of the knowledge of Christ Jesus my Lord: for whom I have suffered the loss of all things, and do count them but dung, that I may win Christ, and be found in him, not having mine own righteousness, which is of the law, but that which is through the faith of Christ, the righteousness which is of God by faith (Phil. 3:8–9).

What he had been and done had no merit at all.

Now this doesn't mean that church membership is not important—I think it is. But that's for you *after* you have been saved. These things don't even enter the picture in order to be saved.

DEATH

Q. Our only son, Bill, died serving our country in Vietnam in 1967. He was a young, twenty-one-year-old Christian. Some people say he is asleep, awaiting Judgment Day. Somehow I've always felt he is alive and more alive than we are. What happens to a person when he dies?

A. Well, may I say to you that when the Scripture speaks of a believer's death it uses the term *asleep,* and it is speaking only of the body. The person who lived in that body goes to be with the Lord—"absent from the body . . . present with the Lord" (2 Cor. 5:8). And Paul, very specifically said to the believers at Philippi that he desired to go and be with the Lord rather than even to visit them.

It is the body that is put to sleep at death. The Scripture never mentions anything about the soul or the spirit being asleep. This is made very clear in 1 Thessalonians 4:13–18 and also Philippians 1:21–23. The body of the Christian at death is put into the grave, but his spirit goes to be with the Lord. That is the teaching of the Word of God.

So your son who was a Christian is with the Lord. You are right, he is better off than you are and more alive than you are today.

DEMONS

Q. According to the Bible, what are demons?

A. Let's turn to Ephesians 6:12 for our answer: "For we wrestle not against flesh and blood, but against principalities, against powers, against the rulers of the darkness of this world, against spiritual wickedness in high places."

The enemy whom the Christian is to fight is *not* flesh and blood. The enemy is spiritual, and the warfare is spiritual. That is why we need spiritual power. The flesh of the believer is not the enemy to be fought. The believer is to reckon the flesh dead and *yield* to God.

There is a demonic world around us which is manifesting itself at the present hour. If I had said this when I was a young preacher, many would not have believed it. Or they would have said as did one dear lady, "Dr. McGee, you sound positively spooky." Today, however, demonism and Satan worship are popular subjects and plainly exhibited. We have the Church of Satan in many of our cities. There are strange things happening in these weird, way-out groups. A man said to me recently, "Dr. McGee, this thing is real today." Who said it wasn't real? If you are an unbeliever in this area, open your eyes and see what is happening about us. People are being ensnared and led into all kinds of occult practices. There are spiritual forces working in the world, evil forces working against the church, working against the believer, against God, against Christ. Don't try to pooh-pooh these things. It is happening, and you and I alone are no match for it.

These powers are organized. *Principalities* are the demons who have the oversight of nations. They would correspond to the rank of generals. *Powers* are the privates, demons wanting to possess human beings. The *rulers of the darkness of this world* are those demons who have charge of Satan's worldly business. *Spiritual wickedness in high places* are the demons in the heavenlies who have charge of religion.

Satan has well-organized groups, and his organization is manipulating this world right now. The heartbreak, the heartache, the suffering, the tragedies of life are the work of Satan in the background. He is the cause of the great problems that are in the world today.

We have the enemy located and identified. That enemy is spiritual. It is Satan who heads up his demonic forces. Now we need to recognize where the battle is. I think the church has largely lost sight of the spiritual battle. We feel that if we have a lovely church building and are attracting crowds and if the finances are coming in, everything is going nicely. The financial condition of a church, however, is not the location of the battle. I will grant that if a church which has been supporting itself begins to get into debt, it is an indication that something is wrong—the battle is being lost in the spiritual realm. There should be questions such as: Are the members of the church being built up in Christ? Is the Word of God being taught? Is there a spirit of love and cooperation among the members? Is gossip reduced to a minimum? There must not be an exercise in legalism but an exercise in right relationships among those who are brethren in Christ. Where there is a spirit of criticism, bitterness, and hatred, the Spirit of God cannot work.

Churches like to talk about the numbers who come to Christ. They like to talk about how many decisions they have had. Yet when the facts are boiled down and examined and you look for the so-called converts two years later, you often find that they have disappeared. We don't seem to realize that there is spiritual warfare being carried on today and that people need to be grounded in the Word of God. By manifestations of demonic power people are being blinded and carried away into all kinds of cults and religions and occult beliefs. As a result of all this, the Word of God sinks into insignificance in such churches and organizations. This is the work of the enemy, Satan, and his demonic hosts.

Q. What is "demon possession"? Does it still happen today?

A. The experience of our Lord Jesus at Gadara gives us some valuable insights. "And when he was come to the other side into the country of the Gergesenes, there met him two possessed with devils, coming out of the tombs, exceeding fierce, so that no man might pass by that way" (Matt. 8:28). Here Jesus is in Gadara, as it is called today. When Jesus entered this country He was met by two men possessed with devils. "Devils" is an unfortunate translation; there is only one devil, Satan himself. The word properly and literally is *demons*. These were dangerous, demon-possessed men.

> *And, behold, they cried out, saying, What have we to do with thee, Jesus, thou Son of God? art thou come hither to torment us before the time? And there was a good way off from them an herd of many swine feeding. So the devils besought him, saying, If thou cast us out, suffer us to go*

*away into the herd of swine. And he said unto
them, Go. And when they were come out, they
went into the herd of swine: and, behold, the
whole herd of swine ran violently down a steep
place into the sea, and perished in the waters*
(Matt. 8:29–32).

This miracle opens up a tremendous area that, unfortunately, we know so little about today. It is difficult for us to understand the import of this miracle because of our lack of understanding of demons. Personally, I believe the miracles involving demons are the greatest Jesus performed.

For some reason these demons wanted to be brought into physical reality. They were even satisfied to indwell a herd of swine. But the pigs would rather die than have the demons possess them! Mankind is a little different. There were real manifestations of the supernatural during the time of Moses, during the time of Elijah, and during the time of the Lord Jesus. Today, however, we seem to be moving into a time when we are seeing more and more manifestations of the demonic. Many instances are difficult to pinpoint, and there is always the danger of going overboard and saying, "I believe So-and-so is demon possessed." We need to be wary of doing this because it is like witch-hunting. Nevertheless, there are many demon-possessed people today.

When I was in college, I attempted to major in abnormal psychology. I knew a man, a medical doctor and a Christian, who worked with abnormal people, and he told me that he was fairly sure that many of his cases were actually in the realm of the supernatural, cases of demon possession.

END TIMES

Q. Over the years I've heard many people say they know who the Antichrist is. Will Christians living at the time of the Antichrist be able to identify him before the Rapture?

A. Antichrist has more aliases than any person I know of. He has thirty names revealed in the pages of Scripture, in addition to many figures of speech. Scripture pinpoints some means of identifying Antichrist and the time of his appearing. I think that the time he appears is the all-important question.

Let's look at the name *Antichrist* for just a moment. Notice first the preposition *anti-* that appears before the name of Christ. *Anti-* has two meanings: "against" and "in imitation of."

> *Little children, it is that last time: and as ye have heard that antichrist shall come, even now are there many antichrists; whereby we know that it is the last time* (1 John 2:18).

Notice that John not only says there is going to be an Antichrist, but already in his day there were many antichrists.

Now how were antichrists identified? By their denial of the deity of Jesus Christ. That is the primary definition of Antichrist:

> *Who is a liar but he that denieth that Jesus is the Christ? He is antichrist, that denieth the Father and the Son* (1 John 2:22).

> *And every spirit that confesseth not that Jesus Christ is come in the flesh is not of God; and this is that spirit of antichrist, whereby ye have heard that it should come; and even now already is it in the world* (1 John 4:3).

I don't want to be ugly, but every preacher who denies the deity of Christ is an antichrist, but not *the* Antichrist. You are antichrist when you deny the deity of Christ; you are an enemy of Jesus Christ. The Lord Jesus Himself, you remember, said that many would come in His name and they would deceive many. And John says: "And this is that spirit of antichrist, whereof ye have heard that it should come; and even now already is it in the world" (1 John 4:3).

For many deceivers are entered into the world, who confess not that Jesus Christ is come in the flesh. This is a deceiver and an antichrist (2 John 1:7).

He pretends to be Christ; he is an enemy of Christ and a deceiver.

Q. The Bible says that Jesus died for our sins, yet we must still stand before the throne of judgment one day. How do you reconcile these two points?

A. We who are trusting Christ as our Savior are not to be judged for our sins when we come before Christ. We will never go before the Great White Throne of Judgment where the lost are brought to be judged (see Rev. 20:11–15). There the lost are judged by their works, and their good works cannot save them. But a Christian has passed from death into life. The judgment is behind him because Christ bore that judgment when He died on the cross. Now that pertains to salvation.

But, you see, a Christian is going to be judged for his *works* to see whether he is going to receive a reward or not. We are told very definitely that we all are going to appear before Him: "For we must all appear before the judgment seat of Christ" (2 Cor. 5:10).

Even the word used here is different. The word for *judgment seat* is *bema*. In the city of Corinth there was a place where the judges sat to judge daily minor crimes. That judgment seat has been excavated, and it is in Corinth today—I have actually stood on it. Paul is saying to the believers in Corinth that we must all go before the judgment seat of Christ, that is, the *bema*. When He comes we are to appear before Him. And why? Well, "that every one may receive the things done in his body, according to that he hath done, whether it be good or bad" (2 Cor. 5:10). In other words, we will be judged to see whether we are going to be rewarded.

Paul had made that extremely clear in 1 Corinthians 3:10–15. "For other foundation can no man lay than that is laid, which is Jesus Christ" (v. 11). Paul likens it to a building. The foundation has already been laid. You can't work to make the foundation, the foundation is down. But you can build on the foundation. In other words, when you come to Jesus Christ as Savior, the sin question is settled. Now you can work to put up a building on that foundation. What kind of a building? He says, "Now if any man build upon this foundation gold, silver, precious stones . . ." (v. 12). That makes an impressive building—gold and silver and precious stones! But there are three other materials— "wood, hay, stubble." And notice: "Every man's work shall be made manifest: for the day shall declare it, because it shall be revealed by fire; and the fire shall try every man's work of what sort it is" (v. 13).

What does fire do with gold and silver and precious stones? It purifies them. What does fire do to wood, hay, and stubble? It destroys them; nothing remains. Paul goes on to say, "If any man's work abide which he hath built thereupon, he shall receive a reward" (v. 14). The test will be made of your Christian life. If it stands that fiery test, then you are going to receive a reward.

But suppose it all goes up in smoke and you don't get a reward? Do you lose your salvation? Listen to Paul, "If any man's work shall be burned, he shall suffer loss" (v. 15). He sure won't get a reward, "but he himself shall be saved; yet so as by fire"—just like a fire that comes and destroys everything you have, burns up your house and everything in it. Your works are going to be tested someday by fire. If they abide, you will get a reward. If not, they will go up in smoke. But what about you? You will be saved, "yet so as by fire."

I like to put it like this: I think there are going to be a lot of people in heaven who are going to smell like they were bought at a fire sale—they just barely made it, and they will receive no reward. That is the difference between the judgment of the unsaved at the Great White Throne and of the saved at the *bema* seat of Christ.

Millennium

Q. Who will be on the earth during the Millennium?

A. The only people who will leave the earth at the Rapture, before the thousand-year reign begins, are all the true believers—collectively called the church. So who is left on the earth? All the people who didn't leave in the Rapture. Who are they? The Scripture makes this kind of division: Jews and Gentiles. During the Great Tribulation, which will follow the Rapture, there will be a great company of Jews who are going to be saved. Revelation 7 tells us of 144,000 who are going to be direct witnesses for God just like Elijah was. Also it tells of a great host of Gentiles who will be saved during that period. Both groups are going to be here on the earth. But the church will have been caught up to meet the Lord in the air. I like to think they will commute back and forth between heaven and earth during the Millennium.

Q. Which of the main views on the millennial kingdom do you support?

A. Well, I am a premillennialist and a pretribulationist. I do not believe the church will go through the Great Tribulation period. I believe that the church will be taken out of the world by the Rapture, and then there will take place on the earth a Great Tribulation period which will be brought to a climax by the coming of Christ to earth to establish the millennial kingdom. Now that very roughly and briefly is my position and the position of many Bible expositors today.

Q. Why is Dan left out of the list of twelve tribes totaling 144,000 in Revelation 7? This has bothered me every time I read Revelation.

A. As we read that very carefully, we do see the tribe of Dan has been left out of Revelation 7 and that those 144,000 out of the twelve tribes listed are sealed. What are they sealed for? Well, they are going to make it through the Great Tribulation. What are they going to do? They are going to witness for God. Now, why isn't Dan included? I hold the view that the tribe of Dan is not included because it had so failed God.

If you don't have a concordance, borrow one from your pastor or someone else and look up the word *Dan*. Read all the passages in the Old Testament that refer to Dan. He is never mentioned in the New Testament, but read the Old Testament passages, and you will find that Dan was a very sinful tribe. The people did an awful thing and as a result God judged them. It doesn't mean they have lost their salvation, but God is not going to use them for service. The 144,000 are going to be a tremendous witness for God during the Great Tribulation. I don't think the people of Dan will be a witness for God at all. They failed Him.

Now, witnessing today is different from your salvation. If you have been saved, you can work for a reward. I think if you exercise the gift God has given you, whatever that gift might be, and you are faithful to Him—that is, if you are "stedfast, unmoveable, always abounding in the work of the Lord"—you will know that "your labor is not in vain in the Lord" and that you will get a reward (1 Cor. 15:58).

These other tribes of Israel listed in Revelation 7 will witness, will serve God, and will get a reward. Dan won't. But does that mean those of the tribe of Dan lost their salvation? No. Read Ezekiel 48 and you will see a beautiful millennial picture. Do you see who is present there? Well, believe it or not, the tribe of Dan is present. They didn't lose their salvation, although they did lose their place of service.

I think that applies to believers today. I think that God sets aside certain individuals and does not use them because there is sin in their lives. I'll be honest with you, I think a great many people are not being used today because of their sin. And a great many who are seeming to build great kingdoms—that is, great religious works—today are building nothing in the world but straw stacks which are going to go up in smoke one of these days. Why? Because they are not really building for the Lord; they are building for themselves (see 1 Cor. 3:12–15). You know, the great sin in the ministry today is neither money nor sex. The big sin of the ministry is *pride*. Preachers' pride is a terrible disease, and I think God will judge a lot of us because of it. God does judge believers.

Now, let me repeat that the tribe of Dan won't be there for the witnessing, but they are going to be saved. That tribe may be just a little sorrowful throughout eternity because they lost out at a time when God could have used them in a great way.

Rapture

Q. Does Luke 17:22–37 refer to the Rapture? Please explain this.

A. First of all, this is part of the Olivet Discourse that you will find in Matthew 24 and 25. I suggest that you refer to the exegetical books that we have on Matthew, as they have a detailed account of this particular section. Let's read a portion of these verses from Luke 17:

> *Even thus shall it be in the day when the Son of man is revealed. In that day, he which shall be upon the housetop, and his stuff in the house, let him not come down to take it away: and he that is in the field, let him likewise not return back. Remember Lot's wife. Whosoever shall seek to save his life shall lose it; and whosoever shall lose his life shall preserve it. I tell you, in that night there shall be two men in one bed; the one shall be taken, and the other shall be left (vv. 30–34).*

This refers not to the Rapture but to the second coming of Christ to the earth to establish His kingdom.

The passage that probably led you to think it was the Rapture is one that I went into a great deal of detail in the study of Matthew where it says, "Then shall two be in the field; the one shall be taken, and the other left. Two women shall be grinding [working together] at the mill; the one shall be taken, and the other left (Matt. 24:40–41). This doesn't refer to the Rapture at all. In the Olivet Discourse, as given here in Matthew 24, Jesus says, "But as the days of Noe [Noah] were . . ." (v. 37). How was it in the days of Noah? Who was taken away and who was left? Well, Noah and his family were left on earth and the ones who were taken away were taken away in the judgment of the Flood. And that is what will happen when the Lord Jesus comes to establish His kingdom on the earth—those who are left are left here to enter the kingdom; those who are taken away are taken away in judgment. You see then how essential it is to put all of these together.

Q. When will the Rapture of the church occur? I know that you believe in the Rapture of the church, and that it takes place at the end of Revelation 3. I recently came across something that makes me wonder about this timing. First Corinthians 15:51–52, which I believe refers to the Rapture, says that these things shall occur "at the last trump." Could this refer to the seventh trumpet in Revelation 10:7? And, considering Revelation 11:15 and the end of the chapter, could the statement about the mystery of God being finished refer to the church age?

A. My answer is no, and I'd like to deal with this matter of "the last trump" first of all. Turn to 1 Corinthians 15:51–52.

> *Behold, I shew you a mystery; We shall not all sleep, but we shall all be changed, in a moment, in the twinkling of an eye, at the last trump: for the trumpet shall sound, and the dead shall be raised incorruptible, and we shall be changed.*

When it says, "The trumpet shall sound, and the dead shall be raised incorruptible, and we shall be changed," the "we" are the ones who are alive at the time of the Rapture.

May I call your attention to the fact that at the time of the raising of the dead, we are told: "For the Lord himself shall descend from heaven with a shout, with the voice of the archangel and with the trump of God" (1 Thess. 4:16). You don't need Gabriel to blow a trumpet to raise the dead. It would be ridiculous to say that. At the raising of Lazarus, Jesus said, "Lazarus, come forth!" It was *His* voice and, in my opinion, it will be *His* voice when He raises the "dead in Christ" at the Rapture. His voice will be like that of an archangel and His voice will be like a trumpet because it is going to sound loud and long over this earth, calling out those who are His. Now that takes place at the time of the Rapture. That is the trumpet we are talking about.

Q. Does Matthew 24, especially verses 29–31, refer to the Rapture?

A. This person says it sounds as if the Lord is coming after the Tribulation, and she is right. He is coming after the Tribulation. In fact, that will be the second coming of Christ. Let's read this passage:

> *Immediately after the tribulation of those days shall the sun be darkened, and the moon shall not give her light, and the stars shall fall from heaven, and the powers of the heavens shall be shaken: and then shall appear the sign of the Son of man in heaven: and then shall all the tribes of the earth mourn, and they shall see the Son of man coming in the clouds of heaven with power and great glory. And he shall send his angels with a great sound of a trumpet, and they shall gather together his elect from the four winds, from one end of heaven to the other (Matt. 24:29–34).*

When Christ takes the living believers out of the world at the Rapture, His feet do not touch this earth. We are told in 1 Thessalonians 4:16–17, "The Lord himself shall descend from heaven with a shout, with the voice of the archangel, and with the trump of God: and the dead in Christ shall rise first: then we which are alive and remain shall be caught up together with them." Where are we going to meet the Lord? On the earth? No, "in the clouds." We will "meet the Lord in the air." The Lord Himself is coming for His children who are collectively called the church.

But later, when our Lord comes to the earth to establish His kingdom after the Tribulation period, He will send His angels to collect His elect (which in this case is Israel) from the ends of the earth. Many people fail to recognize that the "elect" does not refer only to the church. There are two elect groups in Scripture. Israel is called an elect group and so is the church. The church is taken out first, you see, and *then* these signs appear. There are no signs given to the church. We are not looking for signs. We are listening for a sound.

You get the gospel by hearing—"faith cometh by hearing, and hearing by the word of God" (Rom. 10:17). And one day He is going to call you; and when He does, He's going to take you out of this world. He says, "My sheep hear my voice, and I know them, and they follow me: and I give unto them eternal life" (John 10:27–28). When He calls, we are going to be caught up. He's not coming to the earth at that time.

However, the Lord Jesus will come to the earth after the Great Tribulation. To get His church? No, He took the church out before that, just as He didn't destroy Sodom and Gomorrah until He got Lot out of there, because Lot was His man. Before the Great Tribulation comes the Lord will get His own out of the world. Then when the Tribulation is over He will come to the earth to set up His kingdom, and He will gather His elect (Israel) from all nations of the earth.

Q. Please explain the seven trumpets mentioned in Revelation. Which one is the "last trump"?

A. Now there are seven trumpets in Revelation, and I would think that when Paul in 1 Corinthians 15:52 says "the last trump," he would have said the seventh trumpet if he wanted to identify with Revelation. But he says the last trump, which is the last call of the Lord Jesus Christ to the church. In other words, preaching the gospel is trumpeting it; it is the last trump when He takes out the church.

In the book of Revelation there are seven trumpets. Now if you go back to the book of Numbers, chapter 10, in the Old Testament, you will find that when Israel was going through the wilderness on their way to the Promised Land, the blowing of seven trumpets started the march. And we find that they used two silver trumpets "for the calling of the assembly, and for the journeying of the camps" (v. 2).

When the Lord wanted Israel to get going on the wilderness march, He said to "blow an alarm," and those trumpets in Revelation, friend, are an alarm. "When ye blow an alarm, then the camps that lie on the east parts shall go forward" (Num. 10:5). In other words, when Israel started out in the morning, they started out in an orderly manner. The ark always went before, and there would be tribes on the east that would move out, then the camps on the south, etc. So you have a blowing of seven trumpets described in Numbers 10. Now may I say to you, that is also what you have in the book of Revelation—the blowing of seven trumpets that are going to get Israel back in their land. They are trumpets of alarm and judgment on the earth, but that is the way God is going to get Israel back into that land.

So those trumpets are altogether different from the trumpet that is used for the church, which is the voice of the Lord Jesus Christ. There is no way in the world to identify them with each other, although that is the policy of people who want to put the church through the Great Tribulation.

This is a place where good men disagree. I'm just sorry they don't all agree with me because it would make it lots easier for all of us. I don't want to be facetious, I want to be very honest about it—I could be wrong too. But I'll have to be shown that I'm wrong from the Word of God, and I haven't been shown yet.

GOD

Q. If God is all-good and all-powerful, why is there so much evil and suffering in the world today?

A. The prophet Habakkuk had the same question. Habakkuk walked about in his nation and saw iniquity, evil, injustice, and violence taking place and asked, "Why doest thou shew me iniquity, and cause me to behold grievance? for spoiling and violence are before me: and there are that raise up strife and contention" (Hab. 1:3).

Isn't this fundamentally the question of the human race?

The oldest book in the Bible is probably the book of Job. The question that Job and his friends spent most of the book talking about is why God permitted evil to come to him. *Why?* This question is basic to all questions today.

Now the questions of Habakkuk were precisely this: Why was God permitting evil to manifest itself and run rampant in the nation of Israel? Why does God permit evil? Why would a holy, gracious, good God permit these things to take place?

Those questions are not new. They are as old as the human family. Beginning in the Garden of Eden, the enemy has always used that same method—the "why does God permit evil" question—to destroy confidence in the goodness of God.

God says to you and me many times, "My child, I'm asking you to walk with Me and believe Me." He didn't say He would give us the answers, "but the just shall live by faith." This is such an important statement that the three major epistles in the New Testament not only quote it but make it very basic in their teaching.

Today the world asks, "Why doesn't God do something about sin?" My friend, God *has* done something about it! Over nineteen hundred years ago He gave His Son to die. He intruded into the affairs of the world. Through Jesus Christ—His death and burial and resurrection—the human family can be forgiven of their sins. God said to Habakkuk, "Believe Me. I am going to work this thing out for good." My beloved, without doubt this is one of the most wonderful examples of the fact that the hand of God is in the glove of human events! But to see how God answered Habakkuk, you've got to go to the watchtower of history and look back.

Habakkuk questioned God about the Chaldeans. Well, God judged them. The prophet Daniel, who was one of the captives taken to Babylon by the Chaldeans, gave God's warning to Babylon's last king by interpreting His handwriting on the wall: "Thou art weighed in the balances, and art found wanting" (Dan. 5:27). It was a silent but eloquent testimony that God does something about evil. He judges it, and that very night the king was slain and Darius the Mede conquered the kingdom.

Why does God permit evil? Well, He permits it because He is long-suffering. He is not willing that any should perish, and He has provided a cross, a crucified Savior, so that no one needs to perish. This He did at the first coming of Christ.

Habakkuk's second question is, Why does not God judge the wicked? God will answer that at the second coming of Christ, because at that time He will judge sin. All we need is a new perspective to see the answers to these two questions. Christ came the first time to wear a crown of thorns and to die upon a cross. The next time He comes, He will wear a crown of glory and will hold the scepter that will rule the earth.

Now let's make it personal. God has the answer for *your* problems, my beloved. "Why does God permit this to happen to me?" Is that what you're asking today? Honestly, I do not know.

In Pasadena I stood by a little white casket and asked

the same question of God, "Why did You let this happen to me?" I do not have the answer, but I am trusting the One who has the answer. He has reassured my heart, *Just put your hand in Mine and walk with Me through the dark, and I'll give you your answers when the time comes. But trust Me now.* I don't know about you, but I'm trusting. God's Word says, "But without faith it is impossible to please him, for he that cometh to God must believe that he is, and that he is a rewarder of them that diligently seek him" (Heb. 11:6). The just shall live by faith, my beloved.

Q. What is God like?

A. Well, the names of God tell us something about the reality and the character of God, about His wonderful attributes: that our God is holy, our God is righteous, our God is love, our God is merciful, our God is omnipotent and omnipresent, and that our God is immutable. These names all tell us something about the wonder, the glory, and the reality of our God. Scripture attaches a great deal of importance to the name of God.

The disciple Philip also longed to know what God is like. Jesus said to him,

> *If ye had known me, ye should have known my Father also: and from henceforth ye know him, and have seen him. Philip saith unto him, Lord, shew us the Father, and it sufficeth us. Jesus saith unto him, Have I been so long time with you, and yet hast thou not known me, Philip? he that hath seen me hath seen the Father; and how sayest thou then, Shew us the Father?* (John 14:7–9).

Philip knew the Old Testament. Although he had not seen the glory of God as Moses or Isaiah had, he had seen Jesus and had witnessed His words and His works. He had seen God. In Christ there is a much greater revelation of God than in anything in the Old Testment. His disciples had seen Him incarnate in flesh and had been with Him—in His presence—for three years! Hebrews 1:3 says Jesus is the brightness of the Father's glory and the express image of His person. "He that hath seen me hath seen the Father" does not mean you are seeing the identical person, but you are seeing the same person in power, in character, in love, and in everything else—you have seen all you would see in God the Father because "God is a Spirit: and they that worship him must worship him in spirit and in truth" (John 4:24). "No man hath seen God at any time; the only begotten Son, which is in the bosom of the Father, he hath declared him" (John 1:18). It is Jesus Christ whom we see. We are going to spend all eternity with Him. For those of us who love Him, the goal of our lives is to come to know Him.

In 1 John there are three definitions of God: God is light, God is love, and God is life.

God is light. "God is light, and in him is no darkness at all" (1 John 1:5) means that God is holy, and we know that man is unholy.

Light speaks of the glory, the radiance, the beauty, and the wonders of God. Have you seen the eastern sky when the sun comes up like a blaze of glory? A friend and I once camped on the edge of Monument Valley in Arizona. It was a beautiful spot. We spent the night in sleeping bags. When I awoke the next morning, my friend was standing there, watching as the dawn was breaking. I asked him what he was doing up so early, and he made this statement: "I am watching God create a new day." Oh, what a thrill it was to be there and watch God create a new day!

Another characteristic of light is that it is self-revealing. Light can be seen, but it diffuses itself. It illuminates the darkness. Light reveals flaws and impurity.

Also light speaks of the white purity of God and the stainless holiness of God. God moves without making a shadow because He is light. He is pure. The light of the sun is actually the catharsis of the earth. It not only gives light, it is also a great cleanser.

Light also guides us. It points out the path. Light on

the horizon leads us to take courage and keep moving on. God is light.

The light and holiness of God are in direct conflict with the evil darkness and chaos of the world.

God is love. "He that loveth not knoweth not God; for God is love" (1 John 4:8).

John says here and again in verse 16, "God is love." How does God love you? Well, you won't find that love in nature, but you will find there a bloody tooth and a sharp claw—that is what nature reveals to us. You will find the love of God at Calvary. "In this was manifested the love of God toward us, because that God sent his only begotten Son into the world, that we might live through him" (1 John 4:9). God has proven His love. He laid down His life for us, and that is the proof of His love.

God is life. "This is the record, that God hath given to us eternal life, and this life is in his Son" (1 John 5:11). Eternal life is to have Christ. It boils down to this one point. This is the gospel in a nutshell. This is the simplest test that can be made. "He that hath the Son hath life; and he that hath not the Son of God hath not life" (1 John 5:12). Do you believe the record that He gave? He says that if you have the Son, you have life.

This is the reason John has written this epistle—"that ye may know that ye have eternal life"(1 John 5:13). This was also the purpose of the gospel which John wrote: "And many other signs truly did Jesus in the presence of his disciples, which are not written in this book: but these are written [John didn't write everything, just certain things], that ye might believe that Jesus is the Christ, the Son of God [that's who He is]; and that believing ye might have life through his name" (John 20:30–31).

If you have the Son, you have life—John wants you to know that, and you honor God when you know it. It simply means that you are not making God a liar, but you're trusting Him. It is not a matter of how much faith you have or how you feel about it, it is whether or not you trust Christ. That's all-important.

Q. Someone from another church told me that the word *trinity* is not in the Bible and was made up by the early church. Now I am confused. Is the doctrine of the Trinity true? Where is it in the Bible?

A. I hasten to say that the word *trinity* is not used in Scripture. But neither is the word *millennium* in the Bible. Athough the word *millennium* does not appear in the Bible, it certainly teaches what the Bible presents as the thousand-year reign of Christ on earth. Not only *trinity* but *triune* are words used to designate the three persons of the Godhead. They are words of convenience. It is not necessary to have the word, since that which the word signifies is taught throughout the Scripture.

The verse of Scripture that is probably the greatest doctrinal statement in the Old Testament is found in the sixth chapter of the book of Deuteronomy: "Hear, O Israel: The LORD our God is one LORD" (v. 4). A literal translation would be, "Hear, O Israel: The LORD our plural God is one God." The word *one* is *echod*, the same word used in Genesis 2:24 when God said concerning Adam and Eve, "And they shall be one flesh." Two persons—one. "The LORD" is the Hebrew tetragram transliterated *YHWH* or *JHVH*, translated in English as Jehovah. "God" is the translation for *Elohim*, a plural word. In the Hebrew language a noun is singular, dual, or plural. When it is plural, but no number is given, one can assume it to be three. This is, therefore, a reference to the Trinity and could be translated, "Hear, O Israel: Jehovah our Trinity is one Jehovah." Scripture, you see, teaches the Trinity.

The Old Testament repeatedly declares the plurality of God. If you go back to the first chapter of Genesis, you will see this again. God said:

> Let us make man in our image, after our likeness:
> and let them have dominion over the fish of the
> sea, and over the fowl of the air, and over the cat-
> tle, and over all the earth, and over every creeping

> thing that creepeth upon the earth. So God cre-
> ated man in his own image, in the image of God
> created he him; male and female created he them
> (Gen. 1:26–27).

Notice that God said, "Let us make man in our image," using the plural.

At the Tower of Babel God said: "Go to, let us go down, and there confound their language, that they may not understand one another's speech. So the LORD scattered them abroad from thence upon the face of all the earth: and they left off to build the city" (Gen. 11:7–8). We see here that the LORD scattered them, but He said, "Let us go down." The Trinity came down, but He is one God.

Isaiah said: "Also I heard the voice of the Lord, saying, Whom shall I send, and who will go for us? Then said I, Here am I; send me" (Isa. 6:8). Before this, when Isaiah had gone into the temple, he had heard the seraphim saying, "Holy, holy, holy"—not twice, not four times, but three times—it was a praise to the triune God: Holy is the Father, holy is the Son, and holy is the Spirit.

Again in Ecclesiastes, chapter 12, we read the familiar words, "Remember now thy Creator in the days of thy youth" (v. 1). The word *Creator* is *Boreacho* which means *Creators*, plural. Remember now thy Creators, thy Trinity—for the Trinity is involved in creation, as you well know. We are told that God the Father was the Creator: "In the beginning God created." Both the Gospel of John (1:3) and the epistle to the Colossians (1:16) tell us that the Lord Jesus Christ was the Creator. Also we are told that the Holy Spirit of God was the Creator: "The Spirit of God moved upon the face of the waters" (Gen. 1:2). Thus it is evident that the Trinity was involved in creation just as the Trinity is involved in redemption.

The record in the Gospels of the baptism of the Lord Jesus Christ graphically presents the Trinity (see Matt. 3; Mark 1; Luke 3; John 1). At the time the Lord Jesus was baptized, John the Baptist saw the Holy Spirit as a dove coming upon Jesus, and the voice of the Father from heaven spoke saying, "Thou art my beloved Son, in whom I am well pleased" (Mark 1:11). The Trinity—the Father, Son, and Holy Spirit—is clearly brought before us on this occasion.

Again, in the baptismal formula which Jesus gave to His apostles when He sent them out, He said, "Go ye therefore, and teach all nations, baptizing them in the name of the Father, and of the Son, and of the Holy Ghost" (Matt. 28:19).

Paul, in the apostolic benediction, includes the three persons of the Godhead: "The grace of the Lord Jesus Christ, and the love of God, and the communion of the Holy Ghost, be with you all. Amen" (2 Cor. 13:14).

The Lord Jesus taught His disciples the doctrine of the Trinity: "And I will pray the Father, and he shall give you another Comforter [like I am, on the same par with me], that he may abide with you for ever" (John 14:16).

What do we mean by the Trinity? We mean three persons in the Godhead. In the Westminster Confession of Faith the question is asked: "How many persons are there in the Godhead?" The answer is: "There are three persons in the Godhead: the Father, the Son and the Holy Ghost; and these three are one God, the same in substance, equal in power and glory." That definition is the finest you can find.

GUIDANCE

Q. Does God have a will for my life, and how can I tell what He wants me to do?

A. A lot of people pray to know God's will for their lives so they can decide whether they want to do it or not. Well, it doesn't work that way! And a great many people today think, *Yes, God can save me only through faith in Christ, but after He has saved me, He expects me to live for Him. So I'll grit my teeth, I'll pull myself up by my bootstraps, and I'll keep the Ten Commandments.* My friend, you never kept them before you were saved, and you will never keep them afterward in your own strength. If you began in the Spirit, and God saved you by the power of the Holy Spirit revealing Christ to you, then by the power of the Holy Spirit you are to live for God.

You cannot live the Christian life. You cannot show me a verse of Scripture where God asks you to live the Christian life! There are a lot of believers who are super pious and think they are living the Christian life. Yet they are carrying animosity, bitterness, and hatred in their hearts. My friend, that is all hypocrisy.

God has made a way for us to live the Christian life. Again, it is so simple that most of us miss it. We keep stumbling along trying to live like Christians by our own efforts. God's plan and program is by *yielding*:

> *Neither yield ye your members as instruments of unrighteousness unto sin: but yield yourselves unto God, as those that are alive from the dead, and your members as instruments of righteousness unto God* (Rom. 6:13).

To yield to God is a definite act of the will. It is not something that is done when you are out of gear—this flabby, emotional sort of thing. It is when you actively, objectively, definitely, and positively go to Him and yield yourself to Him. This is necessary not only to live the Christian life, it is the only way to truly serve God. "I beseech you therefore, brethren, by the mercies of God, that ye present [yield] your bodies a living sacrifice, holy, acceptable unto God, which is your reasonable service" (Rom. 12:1).

My beloved, it is only as you and I yield and our will moves out of the way that the Spirit of God can move in and bring God's will to bear in our lives.

May I be personal? It has been my privilege to preach the Word of God for over forty years. However, before I stand behind a pulpit I do two things. First of all, I tell the Lord,

"I can't do it." If that were the end of it, I'd never enter a pulpit. I'd go out the back door. But He has told me, "I don't ask you to do it. In fact, if you do it, I don't want it! You let Me do it through you." The second thing I do is yield myself to Him. That is all He asks.

"Trust in the LORD with all thine heart; and lean not unto thine own understanding. In all thy ways acknowledge him, and he shall direct thy paths" (Prov. 3:5–6). These verses are directed to the one who diligently studies the Word of God, to the person who listens to God's law. As Paul wrote to Timothy, "Study to show thyself approved unto God, a workman that needeth not to be ashamed, rightly dividing the word of truth" (2 Tim. 2:15). Having studied the Word of God, and knowing something about the lovingkindness, the grace, and truth of God—holding onto these things—"trust in the LORD with all thine heart; and lean not unto thine own understanding. In all thy ways acknowledge him, and he shall direct thy paths" (Prov. 3:5–6). What a contrast this is to Proverbs 28:26: "He that trusteth in his own heart is a fool." A man was telling me the other day that he was witnessing to some young folks who are in the drug culture. He told a young man, "God loves you, young man." The fellow answered, "I don't need God to love me. I love myself. I don't need to trust in God. I trust in myself." I wish the man had given him this verse: "He that trusteth in his own heart is a fool."

On the other hand, it is a wonderful thing to trust in the Lord with all your heart, to be totally committed to Him. Total commitment to Him is sorely needed in our day.

And may I say this to you, on the authority of the Word of God: Every longing soul who is God's child and truly desires the will of God will be enabled to do His will. God will meet any anxious and sincere soul who has this desire. When you say that He won't, you make God a liar. He says He will. And He will.

What we really want most of the time is our own way, and we want God to put His rubber stamp of approval on it.

But He is not in the business of rubber stamping anything. His will must be top priority for the believer.

HEAVEN

Q. Will we know our loved ones in heaven? Do you think we may be able to visit with each other there?

A. Yes; categorically and dogmatically, yes! I remember someone asked the late Dr. G. Campbell Morgan, "Do you think we'll know our loved ones when we get to heaven?" He said, "I certainly do. I know my loved ones here and I think I'm going to know them over there. I do not expect to be a bigger fool there than I am here!" And I consider that a good answer. Certainly we're going to know our loved ones. The Word of God tells us that we're going to know even as we are known, which is going to make it rather intimate, by the way.

In Matthew 17 we read of Peter, James, and John who had never before seen Moses and Elijah, but the Lord Jesus didn't have to introduce them on the Mount of Transfiguration. They *knew* it was Moses and Elijah. And I am sure in heaven that we're all going to know each other and maybe know each other a little bit better than we know each other down here. So we'll certainly know our loved ones.

Q. I believe that when Jesus ascended He took the Old Testament saints from paradise with Him to heaven. But Acts 2:34 says that David has not ascended into heaven. Do you believe the saints of the Old Testament are now with Jesus?

A. Yes, because Ephesians 4:8–12 says when Jesus ascended, He did two things: (1) He led "captivity captive" and (2) He "gave gifts unto men." He evidently took the souls of the Old Testament saints with Him when He returned to heaven.

However, paradise was apparently not heaven, but was the abode of the righteous dead before the Lord Jesus ascended to heaven. The Lord Jesus spoke of it as Abraham's bosom in His teaching about the rich man and Lazarus (see Luke 16:19–31). He also made it clear that hades was in two divisions, one for the saved and the other for the lost.

Acts 2:34 says, "For David is not ascended into the heavens." As far as this Scripture is concerned, David at that time had not ascended into the heavens. But my belief is that the spirits or souls of the Old Testament saints went with Christ to heaven at the time of His ascension. There are other expositors who believe the Old Testament saints will not be raised until the end of the Great Tribulation.

In Ephesians 4:7–8, it is clear that at the time of the Ascension the Lord Jesus took with Him to heaven a great company of Old Testament saints and also gave gifts to the individuals in the church: "But unto every one of us is given grace according to the measure of the gift of Christ. Wherefore he saith, When he ascended up on high, he led captivity captive, and gave gifts unto men." Every Christian, I believe, has a gift, but not everyone has the same gift. When Jesus led captivity captive, those who were in the paradise section of sheol or hades came into the presence of God.

Q. Please explain the three heavens. I have heard of the third heaven, but I thought there was only one.

A. The Scripture does speak of three heavens. The Lord Jesus used the term *heaven* when He spoke of the birds of the air. So we know that the first heaven is where the birds and aircraft fly in the air spaces around the earth.

I do not know how much the ancient people knew of the fact that the atmosphere extends only so far and no farther, but the Lord Jesus used the expression "the stars of heaven." The stars are beyond the atmosphere where the birds fly. The heaven where the stars are is the second heaven.

Now Paul in 2 Corinthians 12:2 mentions the fact that he was "caught up to the third heaven," and that was the dwelling place of God. So those are the three heavens mentioned in the Word of God.

HOLY SPIRIT

Q. What is the difference between being "baptized in the Holy Spirit," being "filled with the Holy Spirit," "abiding in Christ," and "walking in the light of Christ"?

A. Well, may I say to you that there is a distinction among all of these, but there is also a striking similarity. Being baptized in the Holy Spirit and being filled with the Holy Spirit are entirely different ministries of the Holy Spirit. Paul, in 1 Corinthians 12:13, says, "For by one Spirit are we all baptized into one body, whether we be Jews or Gentiles, whether we be bond or free; and have been all made to drink into one Spirit."

• This is what is meant by being "*baptized* in the Holy Spirit." It is the ministry of the Holy Spirit which takes a person who is a sinner and has now trusted Christ as Savior and puts him immediately into the body of believers. In the Scriptures that body of believers is also called "the church." You get into "the church" not by joining a local, physical organization, but by the ministry of the Holy Spirit in baptizing you into this one body.

• Being "*filled* with the Holy Spirit" is the only ministry of the Holy Spirit that we are commanded to do anything about. That is, you are never asked to be baptized by the Holy Spirit; rather you are told that you *are* baptized by the Holy Spirit when you receive Christ. But you are told, "Be not drunk with wine, wherein is excess; but be *filled* with the Spirit" (Eph. 5:18). Paul goes into great detail about the results of being filled with the Spirit. For example, it will remake the home. And then in Galatians 5:22–23 he lists the benefits that follow as the fruit of the Holy Spirit when you are being filled by the Holy Spirit.

Now to be filled with the Holy Spirit you would have to walk in the Spirit, you would not grieve the Holy Spirit at all, nor quench the Holy Spirit. I trust that I have made clear the distinction between the baptism and the filling of the Holy Spirit.

• Now, *"abiding in Christ"* is something altogether different. You will find a great emphasis put upon this in a portion of our Lord's Upper Room Discourse. For example, He said, "If ye abide in me, and my words abide in you . . ." (John 15:7). To abide in Christ means that the *words* of Christ must abide in us. Abiding in Christ is not something academic; it is something that is very realistic. It means to abide in the words of Christ, to obey Him. He says, "If you love me, keep my commandments." He is not speaking of the Ten Commandments but of His commandments in the New Testament, and He has given quite a few, by the way. To obey Him is what it means to abide in Christ.

• Now, "walking in the light of Christ" would be to walk in the light of the Word of God. "If we walk in the light, as he is in the light, we have fellowship one with another, and the blood of Jesus Christ his Son cleanseth us from all sin" (1 John 1:7).

Have we come into the presence of God and allowed the Word of God to shine upon our sinful hearts? You see, it is possible to walk in darkness, thinking we are all right. We need to walk in the light of the Word of God. "Thy word is a lamp unto my feet, and a light unto my path" (Ps. 119:105).

Q. After a person accepts Christ as his personal Savior, is there a specific time in which the believer must receive a filling of the Holy Spirit in addition to that which is in him?

A. A person is indwelt by the Holy Spirit at the moment he accepts Christ. You see, there are five ministries performed by the Holy Spirit for the believer, four of them at the very moment the believer is born again: (1) he is born of the Spirit; (2) he is indwelt by the Spirit; (3) he is sealed by the Spirit; (4) he is baptized by the Spirit—that is, he is placed into the body of believers.

But the fifth ministry of the Holy Spirit, the filling, is dependent on some things the believer does: "And be not drunk with wine, wherein is excess; but be filled with the Spirit" (Eph. 5:18). How are you filled with the Holy Spirit? You are not to grieve the Holy Spirit (Eph. 4:30); you are not to quench the Holy Spirit (1 Thess. 5:19). You grieve the Holy Spirit when there is sin in your life—you have to confess and forsake your sins. You quench the Holy Spirit when you don't do the will of God as revealed in the Bible.

And then you are to walk in the Spirit (Gal. 5:16), which means that you are definitely, deliberately, and purposefully to begin every day trying to obey the Spirit of God. Now, don't give up when you fall on your face. Confess your sin to God and start out again. When you do that, you will be filled with the Spirit of God, and you will know it. You will produce the fruit of the Holy Spirit in your life: "But the fruit of the Spirit is love, joy, peace, longsuffering, gentleness, goodness, faith, meekness, temperance: against such there is no law" (Gal. 5:22–23).

I want to enlarge upon this just a moment and say that today there are people who are seeking a "Holy Ghost baptism." What they need to seek is a *filling* of the Holy Spirit. We need a filling of the Holy Spirit in order to exercise the spiritual gift that God has given to us. I believe that if you are filled with the Spirit of God you will recognize the gift God has given you and will know how He wants you to use it. It may be to teach a Sunday school class, or it may be something entirely different. There are innumerable opportunities for service, but to follow God's leading is very important.

Q. Recently we have been having prayer with a group; while praying to the Father through the Son, they also address part of their prayers directly to the Holy Spirit. We have found no Scripture to back this up and would appreciate your comments. Is this scriptural?

A. What you describe sounds very much like what is known today as conversational prayer—a group in a rather familiar way talks to the three persons of the Godhead just like you would talk to the individual sitting next to you.

To begin with, we are told to come with boldness to God's throne of grace. But we are also told that there is only one Mediator between God and man, the man Christ Jesus. We are to come through the Lord Jesus to the Father. Jesus said, "Whatsoever ye shall ask of the Father *in my name...*" (John 15:16, emphasis added). Our prayer, if we are to follow the scriptural method, is to be in the power of the Holy Spirit through the Son to the Father. I do not think we should pray directly to the Holy Spirit because the Holy Spirit is down here to help us in our prayer. "We know not what we should pray for as we ought: but the Spirit itself maketh intercession for us with groanings which cannot be uttered" (Rom. 8:26).

Paul mentions the fact that we should pray in the Holy Spirit. Praying *in* the Holy Spirit does not mean praying *to* the Holy Spirit; it means to pray in the power of the Holy Spirit. He indwells believers, and we are to pray to the Father and through our Mediator. We are to come through the one Mediator between God and man, the man Christ Jesus. Let me add that you and I can't come just any way to God the Father; we have to come through the Son. I have no right to be in God's presence, but I am able to come there because of His Son, because when His Son died He paid the penalty for *my* sins.

The story is told that years ago the son of one of the kings of England met another young Englishman in a foreign country. They got acquainted, and since the young Englishman was going back to England before the prince would return, the prince gave to his friend a note addressed to his father, the king. When the young man reached England, he went to the palace and told the guards he wanted to see the king. But that's all he had time to do. The guards picked him up and threw him out. They did that two or three times, until finally he got out the note. He said, "Look here, I have a note from the prince." And, believe me, the guards turned red, but they took this fellow to see the king. And the king, because this boy knew his son, entertained him royally.

Now, if you and I think we have a right to come into God's presence on our own and pray any way we want to, perhaps we should take a longer, harder look at the Word of God. There is one Mediator between God and man, and that is Christ Jesus. We are to come His way. The Lord Jesus said in effect, "Ask the Father anything in *My name*—I am His Son." My friend, when Christ is our Savior, we are *in* Christ, and we are to come boldly to His throne of grace. Let's make sure we come the right way.

Q. Do you believe that the supernatural gifts of the Holy Spirit are still in the church today?

A. Absolutely! God has given to every child of His a supernatural gift to be exercised for the building up of the body of believers. First Corinthians 12, 13, and 14 deal entirely with this subject. Let's begin with chapter 12: "But the manifestation of the Spirit is given to every man to profit withal" (1 Cor. 12:7).

We have three things here. First, *the definition of a gift*. What is a gift? A gift is a manifestation of the Spirit. A gift is the Holy Spirit doing something through the believer and using the believer to do it. Anything that Vernon McGee does in the flesh is useless to God, and God doesn't want it. Only what the Spirit of God does through us is of value. This is my reason for warning many folk who have natural gifts—a natural gift of speaking, a natural gift of singing— that they should be dead sure the Holy Spirit is using that gift. You must be very sure that you are not just exercising a fleshly gift. The reason so many church services fall flat is that we have a demonstration of a natural gift rather than the Spirit of God doing something through an individual.

Second, *every believer has a gift*. Notice that "the manifestation of the Spirit is given to every man." The word *man* is a generic term meaning man or woman. Therefore, every Christian individual, every human being who is a believer, has a gift. You, if you are a child of God, have a gift, given by the Spirit of God, and you are to exercise that gift.

Third, notice the *purpose of the gift*. It is "given to every man to profit withal." Every believer is placed in the body of Christ to function. What is the purpose? Well, the purpose is to profit the body of believers. A gift is to be used in the church to build up the church, to help the church. It is never given to help you in your personal spiritual life. For this reason I disagree with folk who tell me (and quite a few have told me this), "Dr. McGee, we agree with you—we don't think we ought to speak in tongues in the church. We do it in our private devotions." But, friend, that is not the purpose of a gift. It is "given to every man to profit withal."

Profit in the Greek means "to bear together." No gift was ever given to be used for selfish purposes. Every gift was to be used to build up the body of believers. For instance, my eye has no business running off and operating on its own. It has to operate for the benefit of the rest of the body. And that is the only way in the world a gift is to be exercised. Different gifts are given to believers to be exercised for the good of the church, for the profit, for the wealth of, for the building up of the church—"to profit withal."

"But all these worketh that one and the selfsame Spirit, dividing to every man severally as he will" (1 Cor. 12:11). Again we are told that every man, every Christian, every human being who is a believer, has a gift. God gives to each one a gift that is his "severally"—the Greek means "one's own." Each one is given his own peculiar gift. Dorcas, for instance, was so valuable to the early church that Peter restored her to life. You may ask, "Do you mean that a woman's ability to use a needle is a gift from the Spirit of God?"

It was for Dorcas. Dorcas had a gift of the Holy Spirit: she could sew. There are many gifts today, just as there are many members of the body.

I think one of the tragedies of the hour in the modern church is that so many believers just sit and feel like they have no gift at all. If you are a believer, you have been put into the body of Christ, and you have been placed there to function in a very definite capacity. Every believer in the church should be doing his own "thing." God has called you to do something. I tell these young people who run around speaking in tongues, "Look, it's thrilling to find out what God wants *you* as a believer to *do*. Then *do* that. And you can do it in the power of the Holy Spirit."

ISRAEL: GOD'S CHOSEN

Q. Does the Bible teach that the nation of Israel today is still God's chosen nation, even though it doesn't believe in Jesus?

A. The Bible has a great deal to say about this, in both the Old and the New Testaments. Romans 11 goes into great detail. Paul, when speaking about Israel, wrote: "For if the firstfruit be holy, the lump is also holy: and if the root be holy, so are the branches" (Rom. 11:16).

You may recall that in the book of Numbers God said, "Of the first of your dough ye shall give unto the LORD an heave offering in your generations" (15:21). *Dough*, of course, is bread dough! A part of the dough was offered to God as a token that all of it was acceptable.

The *firstfruit* evidently refers to the origin of the nation: Abraham, Isaac, and Jacob.

Holy has no reference to any moral quality, but to the fact that it was set apart for God. Now if the firstfruit, or the first dough—that little bit of dough—was set apart for God, what about the whole harvest? Since Abraham, Isaac, and Jacob were set apart for God, what about the nation? It all belongs to God, you see. God is not through with the nation Israel.

The restoration of the nation Israel will bring the greatest blessing. "And they also, if they abide not still in unbelief, shall be grafted in: for God is able to graft them in again" (Rom. 11:23). Since God accepted Gentiles who had no merit, surely God can restore Israel who likewise has no merit.

Again is the key word. God will again restore Israel. The Old Testament makes it very clear that Israel is going to turn to God again. As an example, read Jeremiah 23:3–8, which is one of the many remarkable prophecies of the restoration of Israel. Zechariah speaks of this:

> And I will pour upon the house of David, and upon the inhabitants of Jerusalem, the spirit of grace and of supplications: and they shall look upon me whom they have pierced, and they shall mourn for him, as one mourneth for his only son, and shall be in bitterness for him, as one that is in bitterness for his firstborn (12:10).

This will be the great Day of Atonement. They will turn to God in repentance, and God will save them just as He saves us—by His marvelous, infinite mercy and grace.

> And so all Israel shall be saved: as it is written, There shall come out of Sion the Deliverer, and shall turn away ungodliness from Jacob: For this is my covenant unto them, when I shall take away their sins (Rom. 11:26–27).

When Paul says "all Israel shall be saved," he does not mean every individual Israelite will be saved. He is referring to the *nation*. In every age only a remnant is saved. The quotation Paul uses is from Isaiah 59:20: "And the Redeemer shall come to Zion, and unto them that turn from transgression in Jacob, saith the LORD." Each individual will have to "turn from transgression" to the Lord. There will be a remnant that will turn to Him; all of them will be saved. He speaks of the saved remnant as the nation of Israel.

There is always only a remnant that is saved. There was a remnant in Elijah's day; there was a remnant in David's day; there was a remnant in Paul's day; there is a remnant in our day; and there will be a remnant during the Great Tribulation period. I recommend that you read the entire eleventh chapter of Romans to get the full force of Paul's argument. It leaves no doubt that Israel is God's special people.

JUDAS ISCARIOT

Q. Could Judas' sin of betrayal be in the class of Peter's denial? Judas' betrayal of Jesus was planned, I know, and Peter's was not.

A. Very candidly, I believe that the sin of Peter in denying the Lord was just as black as that of Judas Iscariot, as far as the *nature* of the sin is concerned. But when you look at the two men and at their intention, the greatest difference is that Peter did not intend to deny the Lord Jesus. In fact, earlier that very night Peter had told Jesus in the Upper Room, "I'll lay down my life for You," and he was sincere when he said it. He fully intended to do so, even arming himself with a sword. When the Lord Jesus was arrested, Peter started swinging that sword. He intended to defend the Lord, but his defense was very bad—he took off only a man's ear. The Lord Jesus Christ stopped him:

> Then said Jesus unto him, Put up again thy sword into his place: for all they that take the sword shall perish with the sword. Thinkest thou that I cannot now pray to my Father, and he shall presently give me more than twelve legions of angels? But how then shall the scriptures be fulfilled, that thus it must be? (Matt. 26:52–54).

But Jesus knew Peter's heart was right.

Now that reveals the difference in sin. Today, in fact, the court recognizes that there is premeditated murder and that which is considered manslaughter, such as killing somebody with your car. You may have been guilty of speeding, but you didn't intend to kill anyone.

This man Judas deliberately planned the betrayal. He entered into a contract with the Pharisees and was paid to betray Jesus. Simon Peter would never have done a thing like that.

This, I think, reveals the difference between a real believer and one who is merely a professing Christian. A professing Christian will continue to live in sin, while a genuine Christian cannot. Now a Christian may do like Simon Peter and commit sin, but if he does, he will repent. This man Simon Peter wept like a baby because of his denial, and the Lord Jesus forgave him and restored him. One was a child of God and the other was a child of the devil.

Q. Was Judas Iscariot destined to betray Christ? If he had not betrayed Christ would we all be lost, with no hope for sinners?

A. As to Judas's betrayal, that is an "iffy" question. It didn't happen that way, so I don't know.

Here is something you may not have thought about. God is not only working on this plan that He has chosen today, but when He started out (whenever that was) on this matter of man and his destiny, there were before Him an infinite number of plans that He could have adopted. He could have followed something altogether different; He could have made man different.

In the Middle West, the prairie section of our country, I heard of a debate about whether God had made man wrong. He should not have made man with legs; He should have made man round so he could roll like a wheel, as the wheel is the best means of transportation on the earth. Well, participating in that debate was the late Dr. Harry Rimmer. And Dr. Rimmer got up and said, "I come from California, from the West Coast where we have mountains. And we would have a real problem if a man were round and he got up on top of a mountain and started down. There'd be no way in the world of stopping him. That might end the entire population of California. It wouldn't hurt to reduce it some, but we wouldn't want to lose everybody out there." So maybe God had that alternative plan before Him, but I guess He knew about the problem, and so He didn't make man round.

And then I heard a comedian say that man's mouth ought not to be where it is; it should be on top of his head so when he's late for work he could put his breakfast in his hat and eat it on the way. And then he also suggested that God should have put man's nose under his arm so he could just flap it back and forth when he wanted to blow his nose.

Well, that's ridiculous, to say the least, but I imagine that a variety of plans were before God at the beginning. He could have made man altogether different if He had wanted to, and He could have had man act differently too. For example, God could have made man a robot rather than giving him a free will to chose right or wrong. So to say that if Judas hadn't betrayed Christ, man would be lost is entirely wrong because God had all kinds of plans before Him.

Let me say this to you, I do not think Judas was destined to betray Christ. But if he was, the Lord Jesus made it clear that even after Judas had betrayed Him Judas could have repented. After he had come out to the Garden of Gethsemane, Jesus said, "Friend, wherefore art thou come?" (Matt. 26:50). He called Judas *friend*. He said, as it were, "You have fulfilled prophecy now, but it's not too late. I can still call you friend. You can turn to Me now for forgiveness." When Judas confessed to the priests that he had betrayed innocent blood and threw down on the temple floor the money they had paid him for the betrayal, he confessed his sin to the wrong men. He could have fallen down before

Christ and asked His forgiveness, and our Lord would have forgiven him.

Q. How did Judas Iscariot die? Your commentaries pass over the seemingly apparent contradictions stated in Matthew 27:3–10 and Acts 1:15–20.

A. Let's go over the pertinent sections of the passages that you have in mind, starting with Matthew 27:3–7.

> Then Judas, which had betrayed him, when he saw that he was condemned, repented himself, and brought again the thirty pieces of silver to the chief priests and elders, saying, I have sinned in that I have betrayed the innocent blood. And they said, What is that to us? see thou to that. And he cast down the pieces of silver in the temple, and departed, and went and hanged himself. And the chief priests took the silver pieces, and said, It is not lawful for to put them into the treasury, because it is the price of blood. And they took counsel, and bought with them the potter's field, to bury strangers in.

When you come to the book of Acts, Peter may well be referring to the burial:

> And in those days Peter stood up in the midst of the disciples, and said, (the number of names together were about an hundred and twenty,) Men and brethren, this scripture must needs have been fulfilled, which the Holy Ghost by the mouth of David spake before concerning Judas, which was guide to them that took Jesus. For he was numbered with us, and had obtained part of this ministry. Now this man purchased a field with the reward of iniquity; and falling headlong, he burst asunder in the midst, and all his bowels gushed out (Acts 1:15–18).

Well, there is no actual contradiction here. It would seem that after Judas hanged himself the rope must have broken and the body fell down. Maybe they didn't discover the body at first, and you can imagine in that hot climate how a body would deteriorate! Especially if he fell quite a distance, what would have happened? The very thing that is recorded here in the book of Acts. There is no contradiction there at all, unless you just want to make a contradiction. The most important fact is that the repentance of Judas was toward men instead of toward God.

Q. Did Judas lose his salvation when he betrayed Jesus, or was he never saved?

A. Well, let's look at the evidence in the Word of God.

> *Then one of the twelve, called Judas Iscariot, went unto the chief priests, and said unto them, What will ye give me, and I will deliver him unto you? And they covenanted with him for thirty pieces of silver. And from that time he sought opportunity to betray him* (Matt. 26:14–16).

"He sought opportunity to betray him." The arrest had to take place when Jesus was alone, when the crowds were gone. Judas waited for such a time.

Then at the Passover meal, Jesus said, "Behold, the hand of him that betrayeth me is with me on the table" (Luke 22:21). The one who was going to betray Jesus was in their midst. There are those who believe that Judas actually left before the institution of the Lord's Supper. I think that is accurate. Luke doesn't give the chronological order; he gives us those facts necessary to the purpose of this commentary. John makes it clear that during the Passover our Lord took the sop, gave it to Judas, and said, "That thou doest, do quickly" (see John 13:26–30). Then Judas left, and we read, "And truly the Son of man goeth, as it was determined: but woe unto that man by whom he is betrayed! And they began to inquire among themselves, which of them it was that should do this thing" (Luke 22:22–23).

It is significant that none of the disciples suspected Judas of being the betrayer of Jesus. Judas was a clever deceiver. Each of the disciples believed he himself was capable of denying and betraying the Lord, and if you are honest, you know that you also could betray Him. If He did not keep His hand on me, I could deny Him in the next five minutes. Thank God, however, He will not take His hand off me, and I rejoice in that.

> *And he answered and said, He that dippeth his hand with me in the dish, the same shall betray me. The Son of man goeth as it is written of him: but woe unto that man by whom the Son of man is betrayed! it had been good for that man if he had not been born. Then Judas, which betrayed him, answered and said, Master, is it I? He said unto him, Thou hast said* (Matt. 26:23–25).

It is interesting to note that Judas did not call Him Lord as the other disciples did (see v. 22). At this juncture Judas left the room, according to John's record: "He then having received the sop went immediately out: and it was night" (John 13:30).

Later at the Garden of Gethsemane, after His agony, Jesus awoke His sleeping disciples: "Rise, let us be going: behold, he is at hand that doth betray me. And while he yet spake, lo, Judas, one of the twelve, came, and with him a great multitude with swords and staves, from the chief priests and elders of the people" (Matt. 26:46–47).

The fact that Judas, and also the enemies of Jesus, had witnessed many miracles makes them realize that Jesus has supernatural power and that He might use it. So when they come to arrest Him, they bring a whole crowd of armed men. Possibly the whole guard came to arrest Him.

"Now he that betrayed him gave them a sign, saying, Whomsoever I shall kiss, that same is he: hold him fast" (Matt. 26:48). That hot kiss of betrayal is one of the worst things in recorded history. "And forthwith he came to Jesus, and said, Hail, master; and kissed him. And Jesus said unto him, Friend, wherefore art thou come? Then came they, and laid hands on Jesus, and took him" (Matt. 26:49–50). Actually, a kiss can either be a sign of acceptance or rejection (see Ps. 2:12). In this instance Judas bestowed a kiss of betrayal upon the Lord Jesus, one of the most despicable acts of man.

Some theologians contend that Judas was predestined to betray Jesus and could do nothing else. I believe Judas made up his own mind to betray our Lord and had every opportunity to change his plans. Even after the betrayal as the priests were taking Jesus to Pilate, Judas could have fallen down before Him and said, "Forgive me, Lord, I did not know what I was doing." Our Lord would have forgiven him.

In the Garden as the armed mob approached, Jesus stepped forward and asked whom they were after. "They answered him, Jesus of Nazareth. Jesus saith unto them, I am he. And Judas also, which betrayed him, stood with them" (John 18:5). I don't want to pass over this because I wouldn't want you to miss this for anything in the world. They call Him "Jesus of Nazareth." They do not accord Him the dignity that belongs to Him. They refuse to call Him the Christ. Well, it's all right, because Jesus is a name which is above every name. The day is coming when those on earth and even those under the earth, in hell itself, will bow the knee to the name of Jesus (see Phil. 2:9–11). But now, this crowd will not acknowledge Him as the Savior, the Christ, the Son of the living God.

They didn't know Him. The thing that is strange above everything else is that Judas didn't know Him at first. Why didn't Judas know Him? Paul says, "But if our gospel be hid, it is hid to them that are lost: in whom the god of this world hath blinded the minds of them which believe not, lest the light of the glorious gospel of Christ, who is the image of God, should shine unto them" (2 Cor. 4:3–4). We are told that the natural man does not receive the things of the Spirit of God, neither can he know them because they are spiritually discerned. I believe that Judas did not know Him because He stood there as the Lord of glory. "As soon then as he had said unto them, I am he, they went backward, and fell to the ground" (John 18:6).

"And the Word was made flesh, and dwelt among us, (and we beheld his glory, the glory as of the only begotten of the Father,) full of grace and truth" (John 1:14). Even in this dark hour when He was yielding Himself as the Lamb of God that taketh away the sin of the world, He revealed His deity—and they fell backward! He revealed to these men that He was absolutely in charge, and they could not arrest Him without His permission. They didn't fall forward to worship Him. They fell backward in fear and in absolute dismay. I think there was utter confusion for a moment when they fell backward. They were not seeing simply Jesus of Nazareth but the God-man, the Lord of glory.

This fulfills prophecy. "The LORD is my light and my salvation; whom shall I fear? the LORD is the strength of my life; of whom shall I be afraid? When the wicked, even mine enemies and my foes, came upon me to eat up my flesh, they stumbled and fell" (Ps. 27:1–2). This is the Godward side. Then in Psalm 35:4 we see the manward side. "Let them be confounded and put to shame that seek after my soul: let them be turned back and brought to confusion that devise my hurt." Then listen to Psalm 40:14: "Let them be ashamed and confounded together that seek after my soul to destroy it; let them be driven backward and put to shame that wish me evil." What a fulfillment we have here when our Lord for a brief moment reveals His glory to them. They are seeking Jesus of Nazareth. Well, here He is, but He is the Lord of glory.

My friend, whom do you see? Do you know who He is? The unsaved man doesn't know Him. People may even read the Bible and be very religious and very moral and not see that Jesus of Nazareth is the Christ, the Son of the living God.

In the morning the Sanhedrin convened and made official their decision to put Jesus to death. "Then Judas, which had betrayed him, when he saw that he was condemned, repented himself, and brought again the thirty pieces of silver to the chief priests and elders" (Matt. 27:3). The Lord Jesus was there when Judas came. As the chief priests and elders were leading Him through that hall to take Him to Pilate, here comes Judas. Why doesn't Judas turn to the Lord Jesus and ask forgiveness? Instead, he addresses the religious rulers: "Saying, I have sinned in that I have betrayed the innocent blood. And they said, What is that to us? see thou to that" (Matt 27:4). In other words, "You did the job, and it's over with. We have the One we were after. We have paid you off, and we have no need of you any further." So this man throws down the money, leaves the temple area, goes out, and hangs himself. Yet he could have turned to the Lord Jesus and would have been forgiven!

The significant thing is that Jesus was present when Judas returned with his thirty pieces of silver. In fact, Jesus was on His way to die—even for Judas. Our Lord had given him an opportunity to come back to Him there in the Garden of Gethsemane, and He had said, "Friend, wherefore art thou come?" And even at this eleventh hour, Judas could have turned to the Lord Jesus and would have been forgiven.

You question whether Judas was a saved man. Actually I see no evidence that he even knew who Jesus really was. Judas acknowledged that He was an innocent man but gave no indication that he believed Jesus was the "Lamb of God who taketh away the sin of the world."

LAYING ON OF HANDS

Q. Should Christians receive the laying on of hands as well as baptism and the Lord's Table?

A. Let's look at several Scriptures. "Therefore leaving the principles of the doctrine of Christ, let us go on unto perfection [meaning completeness]." In other words,

"Let's quit being babies like when we were under the Law, but grow up and be mature Christians." Then Paul adds, "not laying again the foundation of repentance from dead works, and of faith toward God, of the doctrine of baptisms, and of laying on of hands" (Heb. 6:1–2).

These were things they did in the Old Testament, and to paraphrase, the Scripture is actually saying, "Let's forget all of that. We no longer have a ritualistic religion. We now have a Person, and that Person is Christ who is our Savior, and to be a Christian means to be in Christ. It means to trust Him. It means to please Him and to live for Him, and you don't please Him by going through a little ritual down here."

In 2 Timothy, and this is an important passage of Scripture because this is where Paul wrote his own epitaph, we read, "Wherefore I put thee in remembrance that thou stir up the gift of God, which is in thee by the putting on of my hands" (2 Tim. 1:6).

I'll be honest with you, I would travel halfway around the world to get the apostle Paul to put his hands on me! But Paul took this young fellow, Timothy, and discipled him. He saw that God not only had saved Timothy but had given him a gift to preach and to teach the Word of God. Therefore Paul laid his hands on him, which those familiar with the Old Testament thoroughly understood. It did not transfer power or anything else from one person to another. The only things you can transfer from your hand to the head of somebody else are disease germs. The laying on of hands indicates identification. Timothy was identified with Paul in preaching and teaching the Word of God. And today when we put our hands on the head of a missionary going out to the field, he is identified with us and we are identified with him; he is representing us out yonder on the foreign field.

PRAYER

Q. Why doesn't God answer my prayers? Is it wrong to pray about every little thing?

A. In the book of Philippians we read: "Be careful for nothing; but in every thing by prayer and supplication with thanksgiving let your requests be made known unto God" (4:6).

"Be careful for nothing" is sometimes translated: Be anxious for nothing, or not overly anxious, not worried.

The reason we are to worry about nothing is because we are to pray about everything. This means that we are to talk to the Lord about everything in our lives. Nothing should be left out. Some years ago, I am told, a dowager in Philadelphia came to Dr. G. Campbell Morgan with this question, "Dr. Morgan, do you think we should pray about the *little* things in our lives?" Dr. Morgan in his characteristically British manner said, "Madam, can you mention anything in your life that is *big* to God?"

"With thanksgiving let your requests be made known unto God." Paul never lets prayer become a leap in the dark; it rests on a foundation. "So then faith cometh by hearing, and hearing by the word of God" (Rom. 10:17). Prayer rests on faith, and faith rests on the Word of God. Now he says that when you go to God with a request, thank Him. Thank Him right then and there.

You are saying, "But maybe God won't answer my prayer. I have many unanswered prayers." My Christian friend, I do not believe that you have unanswered prayers, and I think you ought to be ashamed of yourself for saying that you have a heavenly Father who won't hear and answer your prayers. You may have prayed for a certain thing and didn't get it, but you did get an answer to your prayer.

My dad was not a Christian, but he was a good dad. He ran a cotton gin, and the machine would always be running. I would go in there when I was a little fellow and ask for a nickel for candy. He would reach down in his pocket and give me a nickel. One time I asked him for a bicycle. He said he couldn't afford it, and the answer was no. I can tell you today that I never made a request of him that he didn't hear and answer. Most of the time the answer was no. Actually, my dad's *no* was more positive than his *yes*. His *no* ended the discussion.

I have learned now that the wise reply to most of my requests was no, although I did not think so at the time. But the fact is that he gave an answer to every request.

God has a lot of spoiled children. When He says no to them, they pout and say, "I have unanswered prayers." You don't have unanswered prayers. God always hears and answers your prayers.

When I was a young pastor in Texas, just married, I went to a certain city to candidate in what was considered a strategic and outstanding church. After I'd preached twice that Sunday I was given a call by the church. Then later they had to come back and tell me that the denomination would not permit them to call me. As I said, it was a strategic church and they needed a church politician, which I was not—I didn't go into the ministry for that purpose. But I felt that the Lord had made a great mistake by not letting me go to that church as pastor. Years later, Mrs. McGee and I went by that church just to see it. It had gone into liberalism. Things have happened there that I'll not mention. I said to her, "Do you remember years ago when I thought I should have had the call for that church?" She said, "Yes." Then I said, "I thank God that He heard and answered my prayer the *right* way—not the way I prayed it."

I can look back and remember how I had cried to the Lord. I told Him how He had failed me and caused me to miss the greatest opportunity I ever had. Oh, I blamed Him, and I found fault with Him, and I actually scolded Him because He didn't seem to know what was the best for me! He had shut that door so tight that the resounding slam was in my ears for several years after that. My friend, my heavenly Father had answered my prayer, and I am ashamed of the fact that I did not thank Him at the time. My advice to you is this: Instead of saying that God has not answered your prayers, say, "My heavenly Father heard my prayer, but He told me no, which was the right answer." We are to let our "requests be made known unto God *with thanksgiving*."

Now notice what Paul adds in the next verse: "And the peace of God, which passeth all understanding, shall keep your hearts and minds through Christ Jesus" (Phil. 4:7). This peace "shall keep your hearts and minds through Christ Jesus." There are those who say that prayer changes things. I can't argue with that; prayer *does* change things. But that is not the primary purpose of prayer.

We may enter this passage in anxiety, with worry, but we come out of the passage with peace. Between the two was prayer. Have things changed? Not really. The storm may still be raging, the waves still rolling high, the thunder still resounding. Although the storm has not abated, something has happened in the individual. Something has happened to the human soul and the human mind. In our anxiety we want God to change everything around us. "Give us this." "Don't let this happen." "Open up this door." We should be praying, "Oh, God, change *me*." Prayer is the secret of power. We enter with worry, we can come out in peace.

Joy is the *source* of power; prayer is the *secret* of power.

Q. What is your opinion on persisting in prayer for lost souls?

A. I think you definitely ought to be guided in your own mind and heart by the Lord about praying for the lost. You want to pray in a way that is going to be effective, and you want to pray thinking the Lord's thoughts after Him.

If I may inject a personal illustration: I prayed for my sister for at least twenty-five years. I would send her my books, and she would not read them. She would return some of them almost immediately, but I always noticed they had been opened and wrapped up again. I really got discouraged, and I must confess that I became very careless in praying for her. I actually took her off the prayer list that I had and would just pray for her when I would think of her. But one night in Atlanta, Georgia, when my sister and her husband drove me back from a speaking engagement, I had the privilege of hearing the confession of both of them as they accepted Christ as their Savior. I really pinned them down that night, and I was amazed and rebuked myself for having almost quit praying for her. I would say that probably we should never give up praying for lost souls as long as they live. That probably should be the rule, although I certainly did not follow it.

Q. What is the sinner's prayer? Does God listen to the prayer of an unbeliever?

A. In the familiar parable of the Pharisee and the publican we find the answer to these questions. Jesus was speaking to certain people who "trusted in themselves that they were righteous, and despised others" (Luke 18:9). And in Luke 18:10–14 is the seven-word prayer of the publican known as the sinner's prayer. "Two men went up into the temple to pray; the one a Pharisee, and the other a publican."

This is a parable that is familiar to all of us. Oh, with what trenchant and biting satire He gave them this! But He didn't do it to hurt them; He did it to help them. He said that two men went up to the temple to pray, a Pharisee and a publican. You could not get any two as far apart as those two men were. The Pharisee was at the top of the religious ladder. The publican was at the bottom. His parable wasn't about publicans and sinners—publicans were right down there with the sinners. The Pharisee was at the top, supposedly the most acceptable one to God. He went into the temple to pray; he had access to the temple; he brought the appointed sacrifice.

As the Pharisee stood and prayed, his priest was yonder in the Holy Place putting incense on the altar. This old boy had it made: "The Pharisee stood and prayed thus with himself, God, I thank thee, that I am not as other men are, extortioners, unjust, adulterers, or even as this publican" (v. 11). Isn't that an awful way to begin a prayer! And that is the way many of us do. You say, "I don't do *that*." Yes, you do. I hear prayers like that. Oh, we don't say it exactly that way. We are fundamental—we have learned to say it better than that. We have our own way of putting it, "Lord, I thank You I can give You my time and my service." How I hear that! What a compliment that is for the Lord! Friend, we don't get anywhere in prayer when we pray like that. God doesn't need our service.

The Pharisee said, "I thank thee, that I am not as other men"; then he began to enumerate what he wasn't. "I'm not an extortioner"—evidently there was somebody around who was an extortioner. "I am not unjust. I am not an adulterer." Then he spied that publican way outside and said, "And, believe me, Lord, I'm not like that publican. I'm not like that sinner out there."

Then he began to tell the Lord what he did: "I fast twice in the week, I give tithes of all that I possess." My, isn't he a wonderful fellow! Wouldn't we love to have him in our church!

Our Lord said he "prayed thus *with himself.*" In other words, he was doing a Hamlet soliloquy. (Hamlet, you know, goes off and stands talking to himself—and Hamlet is "off," by the way).

This old Pharisee is out there talking to himself—he thinks he is talking to God, but his prayer never got out of the rafters. All he did was have a pep talk; he patted himself on the back and went out proud as a peacock. God never heard that prayer.

The old publican—oh, he was a rascal. He was a sinner; he was as low as they come. He had sold his nation down the river when he had become a tax gatherer. When he became a tax collector, he denied his nation. When he denied his nation, as a Jew, he denied his religion. He turned his back on God. He took a one-way street, never to come back to God. Why did he do it? It was lucrative. He said, "There's money down this way." He became rich as a publican. But it did not satisfy his heart. Read the story of Levi; read the story of Zacchaeus in Luke 19—a publican's heart was empty.

This poor publican in his misery and desperation, knowing that he had no access to the mercy seat in the temple, cried out, "God be merciful to me a sinner" (v. 13). This is known as the sinner's prayer. He would not so much as lift up his eyes unto heaven, but he smote on his breast and said, "O God, I'm a poor publican. I have no access to that mercy seat yonder in the Holy of Holies. Oh, if You could only make a mercy seat for me! I want to come."

Our Lord said *that* man was heard. Do you know why he was heard? Because Jesus Christ right there and then was on the way to the cross to make a mercy seat for him. John writes: "And he is the propitiation for our sins: and not for ours only, but also for the sins of the whole world" (1 John 2:2). *Propitiation* means "mercy seat." Christ is the mercy seat for our sins, and not for ours only, but also for the sins of the *whole world*.

The publican's prayer has been answered. Actually, today you don't have to ask God to be merciful. He *is* merciful. Many people say, "We have to beg Him to be merciful." My friend, what do you want Him to do? He gave His Son to die for you. He says to the worst sinner you know, "You can come. There is a mercy seat for you."

I have to admit to you that I had to come to that mercy seat. And if you are God's child, you have come to that mercy seat where He died yonder on the cross for your sins and my sins. The penalty has been paid. The holy God is able to hold His arms outstretched. You don't have to beg Him; you don't have to promise Him anything because He knows your weakness; you do not have to join something; you do not even have to be somebody. You can be like a poor publican. You can come and trust Him, and He will save you. God is merciful. "I tell you, this man went down to his house justified rather than the other: for every one that exalteth himself shall be abased; and he that humbleth himself shall be exalted" (v. 14).

Q. What does it mean to pray in Jesus' name? My children are believers but do not study the Word of God.

In John 14:14 the Lord says, "If ye shall ask any thing in my name, I will do it." I have prayed so much for them and now wonder if the fault is with me.

A. Let me say that the fault, judging from what you say, is not with you. Let's take a look at that verse: "If ye shall ask any thing"—note that the promise does not follow this statement. There is a condition: "If ye shall ask any thing *in my name,* I will do it." Now the question is, have you prayed in the name of Christ? And you say, "Well, I thought I did." You say your children have no noticeable interest in the Word of God, and you feel that maybe the Lord let you down or there's something wrong with you. If you prayed in His name, that means you accept the result, whatever it is. You see, although we may use His words "in His name," sometimes we really pray in our own name. We want it our way, not His way because His way may not be the answer we want.

Since I've had cancer and have to have an X ray made every six months, I always pray that there will not be any sign of cancer. I always, though, try to say, "If it's Your will." Very candidly, when I say, "If it's Your will," I really mean I want *my* will to be His will, and I want His will to be my will—but that's not always the case. Therefore, we need to learn to accept *His* will even though it may differ from ours, and that's very difficult to do.

I appreciate your problem. It is very discouraging for parents to see their children not manifesting an interest in the Word of God. All you can do is pray, and you can't claim the promise of John 14:14 unless you are willing to go along with the answer that He gives you. You can be sure He has answered your prayer. Apparently, it is not His will at present. He has something in mind that you don't know a thing about. And for that reason, accept His will and wait on Him, trusting Him to work this out.

SALVATION

Q. If the Jews had accepted Jesus Christ as the Messiah, would He still have had to die on the cross for our sins?

A. Certainly He would have had to die for our sins! It was determined in the sovereign will of God. Jesus was "the Lamb slain from the foundation of the world" (Rev. 13:8). The Old Testament is replete with predictions of it which are fulfilled to the letter in the New Testament. Read for yourself Isaiah 53 and Psalm 22 and compare it with the account in the four Gospels.

Q. I know my sins are taken care of at the cross by Jesus' blood, and His blood will stand judgment for the sins committed after being saved. Can you give Scripture? I know I have grievously failed my Lord many, many times.

A. Apparently, you have been disturbed by someone else about salvation. May I say this? We are told a glorious truth in Romans 8:1 after Paul tells in the previous chapter of the struggle and the miserable failure that has come to him: "O wretched man that I am! who shall deliver me from the body of this death?" (Rom. 7:24). Well, does this mean he had lost his salvation? No, listen to him in Romans 8:1: "There is therefore now no condemnation to them which are in Christ Jesus, who walk not after the flesh, but after the Spirit." That's wonderful, is it not?

In your letter you say, "I know I have grievously failed my Lord many, many times." My friend, all of us have failed Him. And all of us have sinned after we have become Christians. In fact, God tells us, "If we say that we have no sin, we deceive ourselves, and the truth is not in us" (1 John 1:8).

Q. I enjoyed your Bible study on 1 Thessalonians 1:3 in which you said that works must follow our profession of faith or it was only a profession. I am disturbed by preaching which implies that people are saved no matter what their lifestyles are like. These preachers don't advocate a wrong lifestyle, but they say the salvation matter is settled. Certainly if the person is sincere, this is true but there ought to be more warning like Paul gave throughout this epistle. What is your opinion?

A. Well, there is certainly an element of truth in what you've written, and, when teaching Thessalonians, I did put great emphasis on the fact that works must follow salvation. However, when you are dealing with an individual's salvation, even the lordship of Jesus is not the important thing at that time.

We are seeing many so-called conversions that really are not conversions at all, and I think it's largely due to the way the gospel has been presented. People have been told to trust Christ, but they've also been told to make Him the Lord of their life. Now, when we are talking about salvation, let's talk about salvation; works do not enter into it at all.

We need to make it clear to individuals that they are sinners who are lost and going to hell. This is the thing that's not emphasized today. Until a person sees that he needs to be saved *from* something, he doesn't recognize his need of a Savior. When the individual feels that he's lost, he comes under great conviction because of his life.

After the individual is saved, then we talk about works. That's what Paul was doing in 1 Thessalonians and what I was attempting to do when I was teaching 1 Thessalonians. I attempted to make it very clear that *after* he knows he's trusted Christ, knows he's resting in Christ as his Savior, then good works are to follow. Good works are absolutely essential. Calvin put it like this: "Faith alone saves, but the faith that saves is not alone." Saving faith automatically will produce good works.

A person who says that he can go on living in sin just hasn't been saved. We have to come to that conclusion. You say, "Well, you are judging." No, I'm not. I remember what the late Dr. Jim McGinley said: "I am not a judge of folk who are professing Christians, but I am a fruit inspector, and I expect to find the fruit of the Holy Spirit in the lives of those who have accepted Christ."

Q. At this point in my life I don't know how to believe anymore. I really thought in the year 1949 I had received Jesus as my Savior just before my wife left me. Many things happened to me, and I went back to my old ways. How can I be sure I'm saved?

A. The devil knows most of us pretty well. He knows our weaknesses, that is for sure. He knows where to hammer at us most effectively, and he is certainly hammering you at your weak point. I had the same problem at the beginning of my Christian life. I could think back to the time when I accepted Christ as my Savior, but for the first two or three years I floundered. At that time I had no real teaching of the Word of God and didn't seem to have any desire for it. I didn't even know what I was hungry for until I came under the instruction of a wonderful Bible teacher. From that moment all things began to smooth out for me.

This Bible teacher said something to me that was actually the turning point which brought me to the assurance of my salvation, yet it was a very simple thing. You are sitting there looking at your life. Believe me, if you look at your life you can't have much assurance! You ask yourself, "Did I really make a decision for Christ? Did I really trust Him as my Savior?"

The Bible teacher said that he had gone through that period also. He said, "I came to this conclusion: When those doubts would enter my mind (and I felt they were satanic), I would say, 'All right, Mr. Devil, I want you to be a witness. If I have never accepted Christ as my Savior, I'm going to accept Him right now and *trust* Him as my Savior. Now what do you think of that?'"

Well, may I say to you, the minute the Bible teacher said that to me, it solved a whole lot of problems. And do you know what I did? In the next two minutes I told the devil. "Now look, you sure have been bothering me! You have even gotten me to the place where I doubt my salvation. Maybe I didn't accept Christ back there when I said I did. Maybe you are right about that, but I want you to know this: right *now* I accept Christ as my Savior." Friend, that settled everything. Even to this good day, every now and then, I repeat that statement and confess Christ again. Somebody says, "Well, don't you know you have already received Christ in the past?" Sure, but I just want the enemy to know that I still trust the Lord Jesus as my Savior.

When my daughter made her confession of faith, she was at her grandmother's home in Texas. She came into the kitchen where my wife was and said to her, "I want to accept Jesus as my Savior!" My wife took her into the bedroom, and she got down on her knees and accepted Christ as her Savior. It was a very remarkable thing to do, by the way, because we had not pushed her—this business of pushing children to receive Christ is wrong, in my opinion. After that, periodically, as my daughter grew up I would ask her, "Do you really trust Christ as your Savior?" One day she said to me, "Dad, why do you keep asking me from time to time? Do you really doubt me?" I said, "No, I just want to make sure that *you* are sure that you have trusted Christ as your Savior."

So, friend, I say to you today, you may be a person without strong convictions about anything, sort of a weakling—that's what a lot of us are—but right now you can say, "I trust Christ as my Savior and, Mr. Devil, I want you to know that."

Perhaps tomorrow or next week or next year you will have doubts again. All right, then go through this again. Stick with it, friend, you can't lose. It has always proven very helpful to me.

Q. Can a person be born again two times? Please answer. You are my last hope.

A. The expression "born again" has become very popular today. Several books are out now on the subject. The Lord Jesus Christ introduced this expression "born again" in John 3. He was talking to a religious man one night by the name of Nicodemus. This man apparently wanted to talk religion, especially about building the kingdom of heaven here on earth, but Jesus interrupted him to say to him, "Except a man be born again, he cannot see the kingdom of God" (John 3:3). Nicodemus was startled. He thought that Jesus was talking about a second physical birth. Well, you can't have a second physical birth, which is quite obvious, and you cannot have a second spiritual birth either. When you are born again, you are regenerated by the Spirit of God, you are given a new nature that has a capacity for God. Though it may not have the power, it does have the capacity for God and longs for Him and will not be happy except to be in the Father's house. This new nature never leaves you because you are indwelt by the Holy Spirit of God. It becomes as vital a part of you as your old nature. At the new birth you get a new nature, but you do not lose your old nature. You have these two natures contending for priority in your life. This was the struggle Paul went through, and all of us do also.

This new birth also means that the Holy Spirit baptizes you into the body of believers; that is, He puts you into the body of believers. It is an organic union of all believers who are brought together into one body, and that one body is called in Scripture *the church*. You cannot be born again two times; but if you have been born again one time, you are still a child of God, though you may be living in the old nature and be far from God.

Q. I thought I was born again when I was fifteen years old. I felt happy and secure in Christ. But over time, sin surely crept in, and I went the downward path. Three marriages, adultery, lies, drinking. Was I born again? What do I do now?

A. It doesn't make any difference how far you have wandered. You can always come home. The illustration the Lord Jesus used in Luke 15:11–24 was the prodigal son. You are the prodigal daughter, but you are in the same position. Now, that boy in the far country was still the son of the father, even when he got down in the pigpen (he couldn't have gotten any lower than that). He was still a son of the father and because of that he had the nature of the father, and he wanted to go back home. Well, he made a decision to go back.

The very fact that you are disturbed indicates to me that, when you say you were born again at fifteen, you are accurate. That really happened or you wouldn't want to get back into fellowship with God today. I think the average unregenerate sinner wants to keep on going into sin. He lives in it. He loves it. Pigs love pigpens; sons are never satisfied to stay there. The day will come when they are going to have to say, "I will arise and go to my Father."

Q. A person in our church who holds a very responsible position declares we are saved by *love* instead of grace, as stated in Ephesians 2:8; and also, that "according to His *mercy* He has saved us." He says mercy is the undeserved love of God. He also quotes Romans 8:24 and says we are saved by *hope.* Is there anything anywhere that says we are saved by love?

A. God couldn't extend mercy just because He loved—not to sinners such as we are.

One of the teachings that is going the rounds today is an overemphasis on the love of God. One of the reasons that some preachers and some radio programs today are so popular is simply because of their emphasis on love—nothing negative is given. We have a preacher here in Southern California who claims he never says anything negative; everything is positive. Well, if you go through the Bible, you will find that there is a great deal that is negative. For example, the Ten Commandments (Ex. 20:1–17) are rather negative! And when you come to the Sermon on the Mount (Matt. 5–7), which so many claim as their religion, there is a great deal that is negative there. Also, the Lord Jesus said much that was negative. And, of course, there is much that is negative in the epistles.

There is this overemphasis today on love. Don't misunderstand me, love is a marvelous thing, but you ask me the question, "Is there a verse that says God saves by love?" There is no verse that says that. On the contrary, there is a verse that says that God does *not* save by love. "For God so loved the world, that he gave his only begotten Son, that whosoever believeth in him should not perish, but have everlasting life" (John 3:16). For God so loved the world, that He *saved* the world? No! it doesn't say that. If God could save the world by love, that would be His opportunity, but He didn't. God so loved the world, that He sent His only begotten Son that He might die and pay the penalty for our sins in order that we would not perish but have eternal life. God does not save by love; the Scriptures are very clear there. God so loved the world that He gave His only begotten Son that there might be a way made for a sinner to be saved. Love provided it, love sent Him to the cross; but because God loves you He can't simply open the front door of heaven and let you in, and He can't slip you in the back door either. God is not a crooked judge. God is righteous and just in all He does. Your sin has to be dealt with. You and I are sinners—that is something that is not emphasized today.

Somebody says, "But doesn't God love us?" Yes, "God so loved the world, that he gave his only begotten Son, that whosoever believeth in him should not perish, but have everlasting life." My friend, I'll say this, and it is strong medicine: You *will* perish if you don't trust Christ. The love of God is constant and God loves you, but you have to come His way. Remember, this is *His* universe, and if you're going to play on His ball diamond, you are going to play according to His rules. He says He loves you and that He gave

His Son to die for you. If you will trust Him, He will save you. God doesn't save by love; He saves by *grace*. Because Christ died, He can now extend His arms to a lost world and say to us, "Come on. You can come now if you will trust My Son who died for you."

Q. I am quite sure you believe "once saved always saved." But Hebrews 10:26 seems to prove you wrong.

A. I don't want to be wrong. I may not know the answer to some questions, but I certainly don't want to be wrong on my position. So let's go to Hebrews 10:26 and see what it says. "For if we sin wilfully after that we have received the knowledge of the truth, there remaineth no more sacrifice for sins."

Frankly, you could move back in that chapter and deal with other things. But first of all, to whom is he writing? The Hebrews. There were some Hebrew folk saying that they were turning to Christ, but they continued to go to the temple for worship and offering sacrifices. The writer of the book of Hebrews is answering those people. He says in effect, "By doing that sort of thing, you are sinning wilfully. You know now that those sacrifices in the temple have ended, that Christ is the fulfillment of the Law—the Law in every detail, the ritualistic Law, the Mosaic system, the religious part. He fulfilled all of that, and now there's no more sacrifice for sin."

How do we apply this truth to our lives? If you are going to continue to go to the temple to offer a sacrifice that was meant to point to Christ, you are sinning wilfully because there is no more sacrifice for sin. Christ was that sacrifice. On the cross He said, "It is finished" (John 19:30). That ended the sacrificial system. That ended this do-gooder religion we have today where people say, "I'm going to do the best I can. I make my little sacrifice of my little good works. I'm like Cain—I want to bring my fruit of the ground, that which I raise. My, I'm such a nice little fellow,

I'm like little Jack Horner who sat in the corner." And what did he do? He reached in his thumb and pulled out a plum and said, "What a smart boy am I!" Now, there are a lot of people trying to go to heaven on that philosophy today, but there is no more sacrifice for sin. Christ did it all for us, my friend, and when you turn your back on Him, there is no more sacrifice. Don't try to bring anything and offer it to God. Christ did that for us. And that's what is being talked about in Hebrews 10:26.

So I'm sorry to disagree with you, but I'm not going to have to give up my viewpoint. If you have accepted Christ as your Savior and you're born again, that's it. You are saved for eternity. And I trust that you will believe that.

Q. Is the doctrine of eternal security an insignificant thing? Our pastor of ten years recently announced that he once did believe in eternal security but now does not. He says there could come a time when a believer feels that he can get along without God and therefore does not believe. Consequently, he is lost. So he has asked the congregation to come out of the denomination and go independent in order that he might remain as pastor and preach as he sees it.

A. The doctrine of the security of the believer is not insignificant at all. And that pastor does not think it is insignificant because he now wants the congregation to come out of the denomination and go independent because of it. So he evidently thinks it is a major doctrine or he wouldn't make that much of it. It *is* an important doctrine. But do you know the problem with these folk who believe you can be saved and then you can lose your salvation? They never *enjoy* being saved when they are saved. They are so afraid they are going to lose it that they don't enjoy it.

And then when they think they have lost it, they have to start all over and get saved again.

One important point, although this is not included in the question but ought to be included in the answer, is this:

You don't have to believe in eternal security to be saved. What you believe is that Christ died to pay the penalty for your sins, that He rose again, and that when you trust Him, you are saved. If you believe that, you are saved.

But suppose somebody does what this pastor believes could be done? Suppose an individual who once claimed to believe in Christ comes to a place where he feels he can get along without God. This pastor would say the person no longer believes and, though he was once saved, is now lost. What would be my answer to that? My answer is that such a person was never saved to begin with. I believe that if you are saved, you are going to keep on believing. You will endure to the end because you have a wonderful Shepherd who is going to see you through, if you are really saved. I do not think, therefore, that the security of the believer is a minor doctrine at all. Very frankly, it is sad that this man is probably going to split a church over the doctrine. I think he has a right to change his doctrine. But to try to change the church and urge a split is something you could not countenance at all.

Q. Please explain Hebrews 2:3 and 2 Peter 3:9. Do these verses mean we could lose our salvation—"How shall we escape" and "longsuffering to us-ward"?

A. These two verses that you have suggested actually have no reference at all to the security of the believer or to the question of whether you lose your salvation or not.

"How shall we escape, if we neglect so great salvation; which at the first began to be spoken by the Lord, and was confirmed unto us by them that heard him" (Heb. 2:3). This is directed to the unsaved, not to those who are already saved. "How shall we escape, if we neglect . . ."; that is, if we just let it pass by and do nothing about it, which is the attitude of the average unsaved man or woman today. Many are hearing the gospel, but they just do nothing about it. They are not saved and have never been saved. He is not even discussing the situation of the saved. The saved are those who have eternal life; and if they have *eternal* life, then they can't lose it tomorrow. If we could lose it, it wasn't eternal life that we had to begin with. Or, as I have heard it expressed recently, you can't lose what you don't have.

Your second passage of Scripture, again, has no reference at all to the condition of the saved person. "The Lord is not slack concerning his promise, as some men count slackness; but is longsuffering to us-ward, not willing that any should perish, but that all should come to repentance" (2 Peter 3:9).

Peter says to the unsaved person that God is longsuffering toward the lost. He is longsuffering toward the saved, too, but this verse is not talking about that. He is longsuffering, not willing that any should perish—that is, fail to get saved. God desires that all should come to repentance—change their minds and accept Christ. You see, God is not talking about the saved person in either situation.

Q. One teacher on radio said that the unsaved dead will have a second chance when Jesus Christ returns and also that there will be reincarnation. Where is this written in the Bible?

A. That does not appear in the Bible at all. It is a teaching that comes out of the wishful thinking of men. The subject of reincarnation is one of the many things that is coming out of Eastern religions. The belief in reincarnation is one reason why in India you wouldn't kill a cow because you might be killing your great-great-grandmother. You wouldn't want to do that, of course. Many are attempting to give this teaching Bible status. But the Bible certainly does not teach it, nor does it teach that the unsaved dead will be given a second chance. Nowhere are these false teachings found in the Word of God.

SIN

Q. What is the doctrine of original sin?

A. Let me first give you a definition. Original sin goes back to the disobedience of Adam in the Garden of Eden and refers to the fact that we are so vitally connected with the first father of the human race that before we even had a human nature, before we had committed a sin, even before we were born, we were sinners in Adam.

What Adam did, we did. God could put all of us in a Garden of Eden and give us the same test He gave to Adam. Do you think you would do any better with your sinful nature than Adam did without a sinful nature? I don't think so. We might as well accept the fact that Adam's one act of disobedience made all of us sinners.

Now let me give you a personal illustration. My grandfather lived in Northern Ireland, although he was Scottish. Even in his day there was fighting, and he didn't like it. So he emigrated to the United States. Now, what my grandfather did, I did. When he left Northern Ireland, I left Northern Ireland. And I thank God he left. I really appreciate what Grandpa did for me! What he did, I did because I was in him. The reason I was born in America is because of what he had done.

In this same way Adam's sin is imputed to us. In 1 Corinthians 15:21–22, I read this, "For since by man came death, by man came also the resurrection of the dead. For as in Adam all die, even so in Christ shall all be made alive." Now, death came by Adam. And if you want proof that the first sin of Adam was a representative act, consider why a little infant will die when that little child has not committed a sinful act. Well, that little infant belongs to the race of Adam. In Adam all die.

The generation that was destroyed at the Flood was saturated with sin. They were incurable incorrigibles. "And God saw that the wickedness of man was great in the earth, and that every imagination of the thoughts of his heart was only evil continually" (Gen. 6:5). But not one of them broke the Ten Commandments because there were no Ten Commandments then. They were judged because they were sinners. And, friend, that answers the question about the heathen being lost who haven't heard the gospel. The answer is that all men belong to a lost race. It may be difficult for you and me to accept this fact, but you and I have been born into a lost race. We're not a lovely people. We are not the product of evolution—onward and upward forever with everything getting better. You and I belong to a lost race, and we need to be redeemed.

Adam's one act of disobedience made all sinners—not just possessors of a sin nature, but guilty of the act of sin. Christ's obedience—His death and resurrection—makes it possible for God to declare righteous the sinner who believes in Him.

Q. What is the unforgivable sin?

A. Listen to the Lord Jesus speaking now to the religious rulers:

> Verily I say unto you, All sins shall be forgiven unto the sons of men, and blasphemies wherewith soever they shall blaspheme: but he that shall blaspheme against the Holy Ghost hath never forgiveness, but is in danger of eternal damnation: because they said, He hath an unclean spirit (Mark 3:28–30).

Let's look at that for just a moment. The religious rulers were not in danger of committing the unpardonable sin because they said that Jesus performed miracles by the power of the devil. That is not the condemnation. He says that all blasphemies shall be forgiven men. There is not a sin that you committed yesterday but what if you come to Christ today He would forgive you and accept you. What then was their problem? They were expressing an attitude of unbelief which was permanent rejection of Christ. They were resisting the Holy Spirit. That, my friend, was unpardonable. Notice that later on Stephen was brought before this same group, and he said to them the same thing the Lord Jesus had said:

> Ye stiffnecked and uncircumcised in heart and ears, ye do always resist the Holy Ghost: as your fathers, did, so do ye (Acts 7:51).

They were doing the same thing their fathers had done. In Christ's day they were resisting the Holy Spirit, and the same condition exists today—they are still resisting the Holy Spirit. That is the one thing He says is unpardonable.

This is a verse of Scripture that every professing Christian and church member should ponder. The attitude and state of the unbeliever was unpardonable—not the act. You see, our Lord said in Matthew 12:34, "out of the abundance of the heart the mouth speaketh." When a man blasphemes with his mouth, that is not the thing that condemns him; it is the attitude of his heart, my beloved, and this is a permanent condition—unless he stops resisting. This is the sin against the Holy Spirit—to resist the convicting work of the Holy Spirit in the heart and life.

Q. What is the sin against the Holy Spirit and how can I know if I have committed it?

A. We read about the "unpardonable sin" in Matthew 12:22–32:

> Then was brought unto him one possessed with a devil, blind, and dumb: and he healed him, insomuch that the blind and dumb both spake and saw. And all the people were amazed, and said, Is not this the son of David? But when the Pharisees heard it, they said, This fellow doth not cast out devils, but by Beelzebub the prince of the devils (vv. 22–24).

This was a tremendous miracle Jesus performed. It was just as great as the raising of the dead, if not greater. The continued miracles of Jesus in healing and casting out demons convinced the people that He was the Son of David, the Messiah. But notice what the Pharisees said. This is the question of the unpardonable sin.

> And Jesus knew their thoughts, and said unto them, Every kingdom divided against itself is brought to desolation; and every city or house divided against itself shall not stand: and if Satan cast out Satan, he is divided against himself; how shall then his kingdom stand? And if I by Beelzebub cast out devils, by whom do your children cast them out? therefore they shall be your judges (vv. 25–27).

They would never say that their own people cast out demons by Beelzebub.

> But if I cast out devils by the Spirit of God, then the kingdom of God is come unto you (v. 28).

"The kingdom of God is come unto you" in the presence of the Messiah. Christ is saying, "I am here! My power to cast out demons is My credential."

> Or else can one enter into a strong man's house, and spoil his goods, except he first bind the strong man? and then he will spoil his house. He that is not with me is against me; and he that gathereth not with me scattereth abroad. Wherefore I say unto you, All manner of sin and blasphemy shall be forgiven unto men: but the blasphemy against the Holy Ghost shall not be forgiven unto men. And whosoever speaketh a word against the Son of man, it shall be forgiven him: but whosoever speaketh against the Holy Ghost, it shall not be forgiven him, neither in this world, neither in the world to come (vv. 29–52).

There is no sin committed yesterday that the Lord would not forgive today because He died for *all* sin. The Holy Spirit came into the world to make real the salvation of Christ to the hearts of men. If you resist the working of the Spirit of God when He speaks to you, my friend, there is no forgiveness because you have rejected salvation made real to you by the Holy Spirit. The work of the Spirit of God is to regenerate you.

In Mark 3 the Lord amplifies the matter of the unpardonable sin. The Pharisees attributed the Spirit's work to Satan. They said that Christ had performed these miracles by Beelzebub when actually He was doing them by the power of the Spirit of God. You see, they were rejecting the witness of Jesus and of the Holy Spirit.

In our day that particular sin cannot be committed because it could be committed only when Jesus was here upon the earth. There is no sin that you could commit for which there is no forgiveness. Of course, if you resist the Holy Spirit, there is no forgiveness because He is *bringing* forgiveness. It is like the man who is dying from a certain disease, and the doctor tells him there is a remedy for it. The man refuses to take the remedy and dies, not from the disease but from refusing to take the remedy. There is a remedy for the disease of sin, and the Holy Spirit applies it; but if you resist it, there is no remedy for you. That is sin against the Holy Spirit and the only way sin can be unpardonable today.

SECTION FOUR

Religious Issues

CHILDREN: ACCOUNTABILITY
AND INNOCENCE

Q. Why is a child acceptable in heaven before the age of accountability?

A. If you would go back to the Old Testament you would see a great principle that is put down that I believe makes it very clear that the child who dies before the age of accountability is saved. We have this marvelous example in Deuteronomy. The people of Israel had refused to go into the Land of Promise at Kadesh-Barnea and God turned them back into the wilderness. He said, "Your bones are going to bleach out here on this desert because you are not going into the land." But He added, "Moreover your little ones, which ye said should be a prey, and your children, which in that day had no knowledge between good and evil, they shall go in thither, and unto them will I give it, and they shall possess it" (Deut. 1:39). In other words God says to His people, "You are not going into the land because of your unbelief. But your little ones, they don't know right from wrong. They don't know why you turned back, and even if they did know, they had to go with you. They couldn't go in by themselves." This is not a children's crusade, you see. So He says concerning them, "They shall go in, and I will give it to them to possess." Now that is a great principle. Why? Because God is gracious, God is good, and these little ones are going to enter the Promised Land.

Now we have another example in the Old Testament. David had two boys who died, one in infancy and the other as a young man. Absalom, who rebelled against him, knew what he was doing. He was a clever rascal, by the way. But the first was just a child, and we read in 2 Samuel 12 that when that little one was dying, David fasted and pleaded for God to spare him. But when his servants came and told him the child had died, David got up and went about his business. They said in effect, "Why are you not mourning for the little one?" He answered, "He won't come back to me, but I'll go to him some day." In other words, David knew the little one was saved.

But in 2 Samuel 18 when Absalom died, you never heard such mourning. The word of his death came to David as he was sitting at the gate of the city. He took that great mantle of his and threw it around his head, walked up the steps to the room over the gate where he could be alone, and cried as he went, "O my son Absalom, my son, my son Absalom! Would God I had died for thee, O Absalom, my son, my son!" (v. 33). Why? He knew Absalom was lost, and he wept for him. But he didn't weep for the little one because he knew where the little one went.

And the Lord Jesus said, "Let the little children come to Me, and do not forbid them; for of such is the kingdom of heaven" (Matt. 19:14 NKJV).

I have a daughter who is up there. I wonder what she would be if she had lived. But she died in infancy, and I know where she went. She is saved. Not because she didn't have a fallen nature, but because Jesus died and shed His blood for her redemption.

Q. What is the age of accountability? I fear for children nine and ten and younger who have not yet been saved at the time of the Rapture. To see them left here in those terrible times seems out of character with God.

A. I agree with you. I am confident that children under the age of accountability will be raptured with their parents. But your basic question is, what is the age of accountability? There are all kinds of viewpoints on this. In the Scriptures you will find that God apparently didn't make an individual accountable until he moved along in his twenties. To serve in the army a man had to be twenty-one, but he had to be thirty years old before he could actively take part in the service of priest. This suggests that the age of accountability is much older than we are accustomed to think.

I remember as a boy kneeling underneath a brush arbor in back of an unpainted Methodist church in Springer, Oklahoma. A man came and knelt across from me and never said a word; he just groaned and grunted every now and then. There was a little boy my age who also came. His mama was a shouting Methodist, and she came down shouting and the little fellow started crying. And when I started crying the man jumped up and said, "He's prayed through." Whatever that meant, I didn't do it at the time. I believe if someone had explained it to me then, I would have accepted Christ, but I was about sixteen or seventeen years old before I actually made a decision for Christ.

In that interval I have often wondered if I had died what would have happened? I honestly do not think I had reached the age of accountability. God is just in His dealings, and I am sure that in a case like this we can count on Him to do the right thing.

Q. Are children who die in innocence saved? Do they go to heaven when they die? What references do you have?

A. Well, children don't die in innocence. Our first child died as a little baby. Oh, how she squalled! You could have heard her a country mile. When she came into this world I thought, *My, what a nature she's got*—sort of reminded me of her father, poor little thing. She wasn't innocent, but she is saved. She is saved because Jesus died for her.

You have asked for scriptural proof. I have dealt with this in a previous answer but let me repeat a key scripture. In 2 Samuel 12 when that little baby born to Bathsheba and David—conceived in sin—died, what did David do when he heard that the baby had died? He ceased mourning, got up, bathed and changed his clothes, and went into the house of God and worshiped. Then he sat down to dinner. His servants were amazed. "Then said his servants unto him, What thing is this that thou hast done? thou didst fast and weep for the child, while it was alive; but when the child was dead, thou didst rise and eat bread" (2 Sam. 12:21).

In short David said, "That little one can never come back to me, but I'm going to him." And the Lord Jesus said, "Take heed that ye despise not one of these little ones; for I say unto you, That in heaven their angels do always behold the face of my Father which is in heaven" (Matt. 18:10). "Their angels" means their *spirits*. That is, if they die, their spirits always behold the face of the Father.

I understand a man on the radio is teaching that infants who die in infancy go to hell. That is hyper-Calvinism that came out of Reformed theology with a little group in Scotland years ago. They said, "Hell is paved with infants not a span long." That is horrible! To teach that sort of thing today is terrible. It never was Calvinism and never was Reformed theology either.

Q. Matthew 18:3 seems to support the idea that a child's innocence is a standard for righteousness. But what is the emphasis of verse 6, "these little ones which believe in me"?

A. Let me say that a child's innocency of nature is not a standard for righteousness. We are all born in sin. David says that in sin did his mother conceive him. He was a sinner from the very beginning, and he certainly proved it. And the rest of us do too, if we live long enough.

The Lord Jesus, in Matthew 18:3–6, is not saying that a child is innocent and sweet. This discourse was an answer to a question—who is the greatest in the kingdom of heaven? These apostles were like a great many of us today. I think pride is one of the great sins of the ministry and *it is the great sin* of many lay Christians, fine folk in every way except they are very proud. The apostles apparently had that streak, and so they came to Him and asked, "Who is the greatest in the kingdom of heaven?" And Simon Peter hoped Jesus would point to him, and I'm sure John and James hoped He'd point to them. But the Lord Jesus did a strange thing, and this is His answer to their question. He called a little child to Him, set him in the midst of them, and said: "Verily I say unto you, Except ye be converted, and become as little children . . ." (v. 3). You have to be converted, of course, but you have to become as a little child if you are going to become great in the kingdom of heaven. He is speaking to them about a conversion and then about their conduct.

One of the seven things God mentions in Proverbs 6 that He hates is a proud heart. In fact, it is number one on His hate parade. So when Jesus says, "Whosoever therefore shall humble himself as this little child, the same is greatest in the kingdom of heaven" (v. 4), He is talking about humility.

Then He goes on to say: "And whoso shall receive one such little child in my name receiveth me" (v. 5). We are to receive that little child in the name of Christ. And then it says, "But whoso shall offend one of these little ones which believe in me . . ." (v. 6). He is saying, "If you will receive this little child in My name, you will be great; but if you offend one of these that has believed in Me, it would be better for you now that a millstone be hanged around your neck and that you be drowned in the sea." Instead of talking about this matter of being great in the kingdom of heaven, our Lord is actually saying to them, "You had better consider instead the offending of these little children."

I would say today that we are living in a culture, in a civilization, that is very proud. And yet there is more cruelty to children today than probably there ever was among the heathen. Always this treatment is a manifestation of that which is godless. Our Lord has made it very clear what will happen to the one who offends one of these little ones today. This awful thing of children being used in pornography— how can you help but believe in a hell when you see what sex offenders are doing to some of these little ones?

CHURCH

Q. Some churches have elders, others have presbyters. Some churches have a pastor who's in charge of everything, others have pastors that just preach and teach. Which kind of church structure is biblical?

A. First Timothy, 2 Timothy, and Titus are called the Pastoral Epistles because they address local churches.

These three epistles were written to two young preachers who worked with Paul: Timothy and Titus. They were led to Christ through the ministry of Paul. He had these men with him as helpers, and he instructed them about the local church.

The church today manifests itself in a local assembly. First they put up a building. In Paul's day they didn't have a church building. They generally met in homes and probably in public buildings. We know in Ephesus that Paul used—probably rented—the school of Tyrannus. I suppose Paul used the auditorium during the siesta time each day. People came in from everywhere to hear him preach. That could be characterized as a local assembly, and it became a local church in Ephesus.

In order to be a local assembly the church must have certain things. It must have a creed, and its doctrine must be accurate. There are two verses that summarize Paul's message in these epistles: "As I besought thee to abide still at Ephesus, when I went into Macedonia, that thou mightest charge some that they teach no other [different] doctrine" (1 Tim. 1:3). A church should have *correct* doctrine.

Then again Paul said to this young preacher: "But if I tarry long, that thou mayest know how thou oughtest to behave thyself in the house of God, which is the church of the living God, the pillar and ground of the truth" (1 Tim. 3:15). The local church is made up of believers who are members of the body of Christ. In order for them to function they need leadership. Somebody has to be appointed to sweep the place out and somebody to build a fire in the stove, if they have one. Those things are essential. Also it's nice to have a choir and a song leader. In addition to this, Paul is going to say that officers are essential for a church to be orderly. There must be officers, and they must meet certain requirements. The church should function in an orderly manner and manifest itself in the community by its good works. Unfortunately today that is idealistic in most places because the local church doesn't always manifest what it should.

From these Pastoral Epistles have come three different types of church government which have given rise to the mainline denominations of the church. The churches never disagreed on doctrine in the old days as much as they disagreed on this matter of church government; that is, how the local church is to function. I marvel that they could get three different forms of government out of these three Pastoral Epistles, but they did.

There is the *episcopal* form of government. One man, or maybe several men, is in charge at the top. The Roman Catholic Church calls that man a pope. In other churches he is called the archbishop; if there are several leaders, they are called bishops. The Church of England and other churches follow the episcopal form of government. They are controlled by men at the top who are outside the local church.

Another form of church government is known as the *presbyterian* or representative form of government. The local church elects certain men from its membership, called elders and deacons, to be officers, and the government of the local church is in their hands. Unfortunately, the churches are bound together by an organization above the level of the local church, and that organization can control the local church.

The third type of church government is the extreme opposite from the episcopal form, the *congregational* form of government. You find it, of course, in the Congregational and Baptist churches. The *people* make the decisions and are actually in control. The entire church votes on taking in members and on everything else that concerns the local church.

The very interesting thing is that in the early days all three forms of church government functioned and seemed to work well. But in recent years all three forms of government have fallen on evil days; they don't seem to work as they once did.

What is wrong? Immediately somebody says, "Well, the *system* is wrong." My friend, if the leaders of a church are not honest men, really born-again Christians, no system will work. But if they are all born-again believers wanting to serve God, any one of these systems will work. I *know* that because they have worked in the past.

Q. Can a woman be ordained as a pastor of a Christian church?

A. While many denominations are ordaining women as pastors, it is not a biblical position. First Timothy 3, where the qualifications of elders and deacons are listed, is directed solely to men.

The apostle Paul has written, "But I suffer not a woman to teach, nor to usurp authority over the man, but to be in silence" (1 Tim. 2:12).

These verses have to do with the learning and teaching of doctrine. Keep in mind that the women led in the mystery religions of Paul's day which were sex orgies. Paul is cautioning women not to speak publicly with the idea of making an appeal on the basis of sex. Paul strictly forbade women to speak in tongues in the assembly. (See 1 Cor. 14:34.)

The apostle Paul speaks of the fact that there were some preaching a Christ of love, "knowing that I am set for the defense of the gospel" (Phil 1:17). Then he mentions the other group who were preaching the gospel, but they actually were using it to hit at the apostle Paul. And he says, "What then? notwithstanding, every way, whether in pretense, or in truth, Christ is preached; and I therein do rejoice, yea, and will rejoice" (Phil. 1:18).

He said that some were preaching Christ "of contention, not sincerely, supposing to add affliction to my bonds" (Phil. 1:16). And you would think that Paul would be dead set against them. Then he says that there's another group preaching Christ out of love; he would, of course, be for them. But surprisingly he says that he is for both groups, because both preach Christ.

The important thing to Paul was that Christ be preached, no matter whether it was done in pretense or by true motives. It is tragic that at times Christ is preached in envy and strife. He is still presented in that way today, but we can always rejoice whenever Christ is preached.

I am a little rough on female preachers because I believe their office is unscriptural, but, as I have said on several occasions, some women are preaching Christ better than the average male preacher. What is my position? I *rejoice* and thank God that Christ is being preached.

There are many wonderful Bible classes today, and they are largely being run and taught by women. Many of them are in places where there is nothing in the world but liberal churches, and these classes have been a regular oasis.

I like to tell the story of Dr. Ironside who was walking through a park in Oakland, California, when a woman was preaching there. One of his Brethren friends said to him, "Isn't it a shame that this woman is here preaching?" And Dr. Ironside said, "It's a shame that there's not some man to take her place." Now, that's the problem. Thank God, Christ is being preached. That's the important thing. We can rejoice today whenever the Word of God is given out.

Q. Can a man who is divorced and remarried still be eligible for a position, such as deacon, in the church leadership? For example, suppose both parties remarry. Would you feel the husband would be scripturally qualified for consideration to serve as deacon? If so, under what circumstances?

A. I know this is a loaded question in many churches today. They have to face this problem; I know I had to face it from a pastor's standpoint on several occasions.

First of all, the thing that must be determined relative to the deacon is whether he got his divorce before or after he was saved. If he had his divorce before he was saved, then it ought not to prevent him from being a deacon because any sin he committed before he was saved would be forgiven when he came to Christ. And so, as an unregenerate man, if he made a big mistake in his marriage and divorce, well, that was taken care of when he received Christ as his Savior.

However, if the divorce occurred after his conversion, then you will have to determine if he had scriptural grounds for it. That is, did he or did his wife commit fornication? If he did, I would say that he ought not to be put into the office of deacon.

Now, if his wife was guilty of fornication, or if she had been divorced before she was saved, I don't think that ought to enter into her husband's qualification for the office of deacon. In a matter like this, you see, you've got to consider each case separately.

If the deacon has scriptural grounds on which he got a divorce, and the circumstances are pretty generally known, then I see no reason for his not occupying the office of deacon. But if there is any question of a cloud being over it, my feeling is that he could be active in Christian work, but I don't think he ought to occupy a position of leadership.

We today have become lax in our relationships and, unfortunately, there are too many preachers who are being involved in divorce and remarriage, and eyes are being shut to it. I personally feel that we ought to get back to the Scriptures for the preacher as well as for the deacon.

Q. Is there any Scripture which says a local church should not fellowship with other Christian churches who differ in doctrine, such as baptism, or with churches who are spiritually alive but fellowship with a liberal church?

A. When Scripture talks about separation, it is not *from* something but *unto* something. Paul says in the first verse of Romans, "Paul, a servant of Jesus Christ, called to be an apostle, separated unto the gospel of God."

Note that Paul was not separated *from* something here, he was separated *unto* the gospel of God. Then, what is separation? It's not giving up drinking coffee during Lent, it's not refusing to go to the movies or not using lipstick and all that sort of thing; that is not real Bible separation. Bible separation means you are separated unto Jesus Christ. Christians belong to Him. We are engaged to Him, and we are going to be presented to Him as His bride someday. We fellowship around the person of Christ.

I have found that I can fellowship with any person who will meet with me around the person of Christ. If he won't insist that I accept his mode of baptism, we can enjoy some wonderful fellowship. I have marvelous fellowship with some people who believe that you ought to be put under the water three times, and I can fellowship with those who sprinkle. I got out of the Presbyterian church, but I can fellowship with them, provided we meet around the person of Christ. Separation is *unto*, not just *from*, something.

Now, if you are separated unto Christ, you will find that you are separated from some groups. You don't have to withdraw from them; they will withdraw from you. I have no problem here in Pasadena about this matter of separation. I find the churches and pastors that are liberal have nothing in the world to do with me, not a thing. They talk about brotherhood, but I just do not happen to be in that brotherhood. They talk about loving everybody, but they sure don't love me. And I feel bad about that, too, because I think I am a nice fellow! They ought to love me, but they don't. I said that facetiously. If you want to know the truth, it doesn't bother me a bit, because if they would meet with me around the person of Christ, we could have fellowship.

And so, you see, you don't have to worry about this problem that you brought up to me. If you will hold up the person of Jesus Christ (and, by the way, that means you will defend His Word, also), you will find out that you're already separated—they have left you. But those who believe as you do will come to you.

Q. Please discuss the matter of separation for all true born-again believers from unbelievers regardless of church affiliation.

A. Well, I've just done that, I think, in the previous question about whether one church should fellowship with another church. I would say the same thing about personal separation. If you exalt the Lord Jesus Christ and speak of His wonderful person and work, and if you hold to the integrity and the inerrancy of the Word of God, you will find that you will be separated. You don't have to do anything to get separated. If you take that stand, you will be separated. Actually, it is the only way I know that you can be separated. My feeling is that if Christians would stand for the Word of God and stand for the person of Christ, we would not have to argue about separation or whether we should do this or do that. And we may be able to win some-one to Christ.

DEATH: BURIAL METHODS

Q. Should Christians be embalmed or cremated? I have come to feel strongly that both practices desecrate the body and hate to think of it being done to me or to a loved one after death.

A. Well, after death it won't really make any difference to you or to me or to anyone else what is done with the body, since it is only a little house that we live in here temporarily. Paul says, "For we know that if our earthly house of this tabernacle were dissolved [*how* it's dissolved is not that important], we have a building of God, an house not made with hands, eternal in the heavens" (2 Cor. 5:1). I have a building of God, I have something permanent up there, and that's the important thing.

Regarding embalming, it is my understanding that in certain states it is required by law that a body be embalmed. I think the undertakers like to include it, whether it is re-quired or not. Personally, I'm on your side in the sense I feel very much as you do about it. But if it has to be done, that settles the question.

Now regarding cremation, two figures of speech are used in the Word of God in relation to death: one is *sleep* and the other is *seed*. Believers realize that the body will some day be resurrected.

The early Christians had a wonderful word for the burying place of their loved ones, the Greek word *koinete-rion*, which means "a rest house for strangers" or "a sleep-ing place." It's the same word from which we get the English word *cemetery*. This word was used in that day for an inn or what we would call a hotel or motel—places where you'd spend the night to sleep, expecting to get up the next day and continue your journey.

The Scriptures teach in 1 Thessalonians 4:13–18 that the body of a believer is put into a sleeping place until the resurrection because the Lord is coming for His own, and that body is going to be raised up. Note that it is the body, not the soul, that is in the grave. The soul is eternal—it never sleeps or dies but goes directly to heaven when released from the body.

When you and I bury a loved one who knows Christ, we can have full confidence that we'll see that one again. When we bury them in the soil it is like planting a seed in the ground—"It is sown in corruption; it is raised in incorruption" (1 Cor. 15:42). That's why I believe that burial, rather than cremation, is a testimony of our faith. It's the reason I recommend it. However, 1 Corinthians 15 makes it clear that no matter what condition the body is in at death, its resurrection is assured.

OCCULTISM

Q. Someone gave me a book and a deck of tarot cards for a birthday gift. Are they good or bad? Are they sinful?

A. Well, the cards by themselves are nothing—they're just cards. But the way they are used is sinful because their purpose is fortune-telling. They are one of the tools Satan is using to involve the unwary in occult practices—all of which the Bible repeatedly warns against. Very frankly, if I were you I'd put them in the fire. They make a nice blaze, and that would be the only good they could accomplish.

Q. Can a Christian use astrology? An accurate horoscope has helped me understand people better—their strong and weak points, why they act, think, react as they do, which types are better suited for certain tasks than others. I realize the power of God can override any traits, but is it wrong to be aware of what our human nature is or how it operates?

A. We ought to know as much as we possibly can about other people. But the place where you've gone off the track is to think you can get that from astrology, and you call it an "accurate horoscope." I never heard of *accurate* horoscopes! Astrology actually deals with the spirit world which is satanic. And why go that route when you have the Word of God? The finest book on psychology today is still the Word of God, and it deals with human beings. You will learn more about the human family by reading the Bible than you will by following this superstitious route.

So many people are going this way today. There was a time when the average person, an unbeliever out yonder in the world, had respect for the Bible and for what it said. But we've come to a day when the news media and a great many folk in public life, as you listen to them talk, go this superstitious route. They seem to put great confidence in it, and they totally ignore the Word of God. They consider the Bible superstition and the horoscope reliable! I heard of a man here in Southern California who before he goes to the racetrack goes to a fortune teller who reads the horoscope for him to let him know whether he should bet or not. And I'm told that he has about used up his fortune because he did not always get accurate information from his fortune teller. And if he did, it wouldn't have come from a right source, by any means.

If you want supernatural information and insights, my friend, get it from the right source, the Word of God.

SABBATH

Q. Was the Sabbath always on Saturday? Why don't we have church on the Sabbath, like the Jews do?

A. The Sabbath day is Saturday, the seventh day of the week according to our calendar. Furthermore, the Sabbath day has never been changed to Sunday.

The present-day controversy hinges upon a false premise which resulted in a warped and distorted viewpoint of the real meaning of the Sabbath day as found in the Word of God. Many Christians have a woeful misconception of why the church has always observed the first day of the week. Nothing but abysmal ignorance has permitted the protagonists of the Sabbath day to traffic in their legalistic system.

Now this question today, "When was the Sabbath changed to Sunday?" is like the old chestnut, "Do you still beat your wife?" You cannot answer that question without getting into a peck of trouble. If you say, "Yes," you are wrong. If you say, "No, " you are wrong, and you are immediately in difficulty.

The reason given in Exodus 20:10–11 for the observance of the Sabbath day is that God, in creation, did all the work in six days and He rested on the seventh and hallowed that day. Therefore, in Exodus the basis is ceremonial—or, as we could say today, theological or religious—and is founded upon the fact that God rested on the seventh day.

After Christ had raised the man at the pool of Bethesda, the Pharisees said that He had worked on the Sabbath day. Our Lord said, "My Father worketh hitherto, and I work" (John 5:17). In other words, "We are not observing a Sabbath day any longer; We are working!" And He moved into action at that point!

When we turn to Deuteronomy we find an altogether different reason given for the Sabbath day. Observe this passage in Deuteronomy 5:15: "And remember that thou wast a servant in the land of Egypt, and that the LORD thy God brought thee out thence through a mighty hand and by a stretched out arm: therefore the LORD thy God commanded thee to keep the sabbath day." In Egypt the children of Israel had worked in hard labor seven days a week, from sunup till sunset without rest from sorrow or weariness. Now God tells them that because He has delivered them out of the land of Egypt and permitted them to keep one day, He wants them to remember their servants and all their animals. Man and beast must rest one day out of each week. That is humanitarian.

Our Lord Jesus moved into the picture on the Sabbath dispute. You will recall *what* He said to the religious rulers when His disciples were plucking the ears of grain on the Sabbath and the rulers challenged Him because of it: "The sabbath was made for man, and not man for the sabbath" (Mark 2:27).

This is a flat statement of the humanitarian aspect of the question. These two reasons are tremendous. The Sabbath day was bound together with the ceremonial worship of this nation—they never could be divorced. God said that they must keep holy His Sabbath and His sanctuary.

In Old Testament times there were 1,521 ways in which one could break the Sabbath! If they tied a knot they broke the Sabbath; a scribe could not carry a pen because that would be carrying a burden on the Sabbath. A man was not permitted even to kill a flea.

It is little wonder that Simon Peter stood up in the first Council of Jerusalem and said to those gathered there: "Now therefore why tempt [make trial] ye God, to put a yoke upon the neck of the disciples, which neither our fathers nor we were able to bear?" (Acts 15:10). He meant that they had not been able to keep it at all.

When we pass from the Old Testament and come into the New Testament there is nothing short of a revolution taking place as far as the Sabbath day is concerned.

Every commandment is repeated in the Epistles for Christians as an item of Christian conduct, with one exception—the Sabbath day. Nowhere is a Sabbath commandment given to the church. In fact, just the contrary is true, for the church is warned against keeping the Sabbath day.

Now let's consider the second part of your question by looking first at the book of Acts: "And upon the first day of the week, when the disciples came together to break bread, Paul preached unto them, ready to depart on the morrow;

and continued his speech until midnight" (20:7). Note that it was upon the first day of the week that they came together. Where we have a record of the day on which the early church met, it was always the first day of the week. Paul tells the Corinthians that they are to bring their gifts on the *first* day of the week (see 1 Cor. 16:2). According to our verse in Acts, "when the disciples came together to break bread" it was "upon the *first* day of the week." This means that they celebrated the Lord's Supper on Sunday. Paul preached to them on this day. The early church met on the first day of the week because it was the day on which Jesus came back from the dead. Under the old creation the seventh day was the important day, the Sabbath day. On the Sabbath day Jesus was dead, inside the tomb. On the first day of the week He came forth. Christians meet together on that day because we are joined to a living Christ. That is the testimony of the first day of the week.

Now let us read it the way Paul wrote it: "Upon the first day of the week let every one of you lay by him in store, as God hath prospered him, that there be no gatherings when I come" (1 Cor. 16:2). "Upon the first day of the week." If you don't meet on the first day of the week to worship God, then you will want to meet on that day to make your offering, which is a part of worship. That is ridiculous, of course. He says to bring your offering on the first day of the week because this was the day on which the church came together to remember the Lord Jesus in His death and in His resurrection. He rose on the first day of the week, which is Sunday, not the Sabbath day.

SHROUD OF TURIN

Q. Do you believe the Shroud of Turin is Christ's burial cloth, and why or why not?

A. No, simply because there is absolutely no historical evidence that would confirm it. To begin with, there have been claims of two shrouds. One of them has been discredited, and so which one are you going to choose? Both can't be right. One of them was a hoax, and chances are both of them are hoaxes.

The thing that makes it impossible is that everything that was connected with the physical life of Christ has disappeared. Isn't that interesting? For instance, the cross is gone. Oh, I know they took many wagonloads of splinters and chips out of churches in England, all purported to be part of Christ's cross, but that doesn't prove anything except that somebody's wrong. God saw to it that everything connected with the physical life of Christ disappeared, because it is obvious that men would worship such things, you see, instead of worshiping Christ. What is important is the person of Christ and what His death and resurrection have done for us.

SOCIAL ISSUES AND WORLD CONCERNS

ABORTION

Q. Am I right in believing that, according to Psalm 139:16, one's name is written in the Book of Life *before* he is born?

A. Well, let's look at that verse of Scripture: "Thine eyes did see my substance, yet being unperfect; and in thy book all my members were written, which in continuance were fashioned, when as yet there was none of them."

I conclude from this statement that that is exactly what takes place—we are recorded. And then may I say as an aside that this is the psalm I use for rejecting abortion. Clearly, as this verse states, when the members are still unperfected, at that very moment you are a human being in God's sight. To kill a fetus is murder; it is nothing short of murder. The thought we have here is that a fetus is recorded in God's Book of Life.

ALCOHOL

Q. Should Christians oppose the use of alcoholic beverage? First Timothy says, "Drink no longer water, but use a little wine for thy stomach's sake and thine often infirmities" (1 Tim. 5:23).

A. I have to smile when I read this verse because it has certainly been abused in its many interpretations. Obviously the wine recommended to Timothy was not being used as a beverage but as a medicine. As you have pointed out in 1 Timothy 5:23, Paul encourages Timothy to use a little wine for his stomach's sake. Even today many of the medicines we take contain a high percentage of alcohol.

The problem with alcohol in our day is its use as a beverage. I feel that the church should teach total abstinence because the abuse of alcohol is so prevalent. I do not believe that a Christian should use alcohol as a refreshment or a drink.

Paul shows us that we find our joy in the Lord: "And be not drunk with wine, wherein is excess; but be filled with the Spirit; speaking to yourselves in psalms and hymns and spiritual songs, singing and making melody in your heart to the Lord" (Eph. 5:18–19).

My translation puts it like this: "Be not made drunk with wine in which is riot [dissoluteness], but be filled with the Spirit; speaking one to another in psalms and hymns and spiritual songs, singing and making melody in your heart to the Lord." This is not just a dry discourse against the evils of drunkenness, even though drunkenness was the besetting sin of the ancient world—and is still the besetting sin of the hour. Drunkenness may actually be the sin that will destroy America, but this is not a lecture on drunkenness. Actually, Paul is making a comparison. Don't be drunk with wine. Why not? Because it will stimulate temporarily; it will energize the flesh, but then it will let you down and lead you in the direction of profligacy and dissoluteness, and finally desperation, despair, and delirium tremens.

Now people today feel a need for something, which I think explains the cocktail hour and the barroom—they turn to hard liquor to fill that need. If they are not children of God, they have no other resource or recourse. However, the child of God is to be filled with the Holy Spirit. What does it mean to be filled with the Holy Spirit? We can find the analogy in the man who is drinking, which is the reason Paul uses it here. The man who is drinking is possessed by the wine. You can recognize that a man is drunk. In contrast, the Holy Spirit should possess the believer; it is a divine intoxication that fills every need. Being filled with the Holy Spirit is not an excessive emotionalism, but rather furnishes the dynamic for living and for accomplishing something for God. When we are filled by the Holy Spirit we are *controlled* by the Holy Spirit.

CAPITAL PUNISHMENT

Q. Why do you believe in capital punishment?

A. I have a booklet titled *Is Capital Punishment Christian* and I want to say that I do believe in the necessity of capital punishment and I believe it is Christian. I believe it is the mark of a civilized society and that when criminals are not punished you have a barbaric and uncivilized society. Unfortunately, we almost have that today.

I am sure that one of the things in your mind is the fact that the sixth of the Ten Commandments says, "Thou shalt not kill," and some folk say therefore that government has no right to take life.

I wish that folk would study the Word of God in the context in which it is given. The sixth commandment that says, "Thou shalt not kill" (*murder* is a better translation) has no reference to governments at all. The Ten Commandments were given to *individuals,* and to the individual God says, "Thou shalt not murder." He is not speaking at all to a government. You as an individual have no right to murder, and if you do, the government has a right to punish you.

Now these folk say capital punishment began in the days of Moses and that it is in the Mosaic Law. Let me say this, that capital punishment goes all the way back to the Garden of Eden, when God said, "In the day that thou eatest thereof thou shalt surely die" (Gen. 2:17). The very fact that men die demonstrates the fact that God is punishing the human family for their sin.

How did death come? Death came because of Adam's sin, a sin that has been handed down to all of us today. Because we're all in Adam, we all die.

After our first parents moved out of the Garden of Eden, they had two sons (they had many other children also). Their firstborn son, Cain, killed his brother; he murdered him. No commandment had been given at that time about murder, so God protected Cain. A race came from this man, and if you will follow the story, one in Cain's line committed another murder and said, in effect, "If Cain got by with it, why can't I?" So this man, Lamech, committed murder. Before long you have the whole human family that is given over to violence, as it was in the days of Noah.

Somebody says, "Well, God didn't punish the murderer then." What do you think the Flood was? The Flood was a judgment of God. Now after the Flood, God said, "Whoso sheddeth man's blood, by man shall his blood be shed: for in the image of God made he man" (Gen. 9:6).

Human life is so precious that God says no person has a right to take that life. And when that life is taken because of hatred or some momentary passion, God says it is murder and human life must be protected. Therefore, if anyone takes a human life, he'll have to sacrifice his own life.

Today the criminal is being protected, and we hear all about his rights. A criminal ought to be tried and treated as a criminal, and the victim of a crime today is the one who should be protected. God gave to man this arm of human government to protect human life. The way you protect human life is to see that no one has a right to take another's life unless he is willing to sacrifice his own. God gave this commandment to man to protect the human race.

Now you will find that the Lord Jesus lifted that commandment to the nth degree. He says that if you, in your heart, hate your brother, you are guilty of murder and have broken this commandment. I believe that most of us, if we were really tried for what is in our hearts, would be executed. But because of the grace of God, He is holding back that judgment to give us an opportunity that we might be saved.

So you and I today are to be under human government. That human government should have the right to take the life of a person who intentionally has taken another's life. According to Scripture, rulers are not a terror to good works but to evil.

When I first gave my message on capital punishment, the opposition suggested that it does not deter crime. Well, when capital punishment was voted out in California, there was an increase of crime here. Before that, in my neighborhood we lived in comparative peace with our neighbors. We could relax in our homes. But now that has been changed. We are suddenly in a dangerous place where residents lock themselves in at night for fear of their very lives. What has happened? Well, the criminal out yonder today carries a gun because he won't mind murdering. He knows the most he would get would be "life"—which in actuality would be only a few years, and chances are he wouldn't even get that.

California has reinstated the death penalty, but the act is meaningless unless it is enforced.

There was a time when a robber was not apt to shoot an individual. In fact, many of them carried unloaded guns because they knew if they were arrested for murder they would be executed. To argue today that the death penalty is not a deterrent to crime is so illogical and so unreasonable and so prejudiced that to me it is not worth even considering.

The civilization that you and I have enjoyed is known as the Judeo-Christian civilization because of the Judeo-Christian ethic. And that ethic taught capital punishment. We thought we had graduated from it when we voted out the death penalty, but in fact we were not as far along as civilized human beings as we thought we were.

Q. If the execution chamber is a tool to fight sin and crime, then shouldn't we put adulterers, homosexuals, and Sabbath violators in the execution chamber along with the heinous murderer? All of these crimes carried the death penalty under the old covenant of God.

A. First of all, let me say that I do not consider the execution chamber to be a tool to fight sin and crime. I consider it a place of punishment for crime and, as such, an undeniable and well-proven deterrent to crime.

Now, as to putting us back under the old covenant, it would be true that if today there were a death penalty for adultery and they stoned the offenders to death as they did under Old Testament law, there would be so many rock piles in Southern California you couldn't even get off and on the freeways! But they do not execute adulterers today. I have a notion that if they did, it sure would cut down the sin of adultery! The same is true of homosexuals. But as for Sabbath violators, no. To begin with, laws concerning the Sabbath were never given to any but the people of Israel.

But are these moral laws good for us today? Our founding fathers thought they were. Some places even had "blue" laws for the Sabbath day, but eventually those laws were eliminated. Today they are getting rid of the execution chamber for murder, but Scripture clearly states that this law was for all mankind, going back to the very beginning: "Whoso sheddeth man's blood, by man shall his blood be shed" (Gen. 9:6). That should be the foundation of human government—to consider human life sacred.

GOVERNMENT

Q. Is it ever right for a Christian to break a law?

A. Romans 13 has some specific things to say about this problem: "Let every soul be subject unto the higher powers. For there is no power but of God: the powers that be are ordained of God" (v. 1). We are to submit ourselves to governmental authorities for the very simple reason that they are ordained of God. It is true that the kingdoms of this world belong to Satan and that injustice and corruption abound in all governments; yet God still has control. History is the monotonous account of how one government after another flourished for a time in pomp and pride and then was brought to ruin and rubble. Why? Because corruption and lawlessness became rampant, and God brought the government to an end. God still rules, even over this earth. God has not abdicated His throne; He is riding triumphantly in His chariot. Neither is He disturbed about what is happening on this earth.

Now the allegiance of the Christian is to *that* throne. And his relationship to his government on earth is submission. "Whosoever therefore resisteth the power, resisteth the ordinance of God: and they that resist shall receive to themselves damnation" (Rom. 13:2). The believer has opposed bad government and supported good government on the theory that good government is the one ordained of God. The believer is for law and order, not lawlessness; for honesty and justice, not corruption and rank injustice. At great moments of crisis in history—and that's where we are today—the believers have had difficult decisions to make.

I want to give you my viewpoint briefly, and I believe that it will coincide with history. During these last days, which I believe we are in right now, lawlessness abounds. The believer must oppose it; he must not be a part of it, even when it is in his own government. We need to beware of those who would change our government under the guise of improving it.

Yet it is very difficult to say that we are to obey a corrupt government. There is corruption in our government from the top to the bottom, and it is not confined to one party. Our forefathers had a Bible background, but the unsaved, godless men in government positions today actually do not understand the American system. For example, while both parties talk about eliminating poverty, poverty remains because of corruption. What's wrong? Well, the thing that is wrong is the human heart.

What is the Christian to do? My business is to get out the Word of God, and my business is to obey the law. That is what Paul is saying here. Christianity is not a movement to improve government or to help society clean up the town. It is to preach a gospel that is the power of God unto salvation which will bring into existence individuals like the men who signed the Declaration of Independence and gave us a government of laws.

Now let's go back to the original question: "Is it ever right for a Christian to break a law?" Let's turn to Acts 4:17–19 and let Peter and John answer for us. The authorities had commanded them to stop speaking of Jesus.

> But that it spread no further among the people, let us straitly threaten them, that they speak henceforth to no man in this name. And they called them, and commanded them not to speak at all nor teach in the name of Jesus. But Peter and John answered and said unto them, Whether it be right in the sight of God to hearken unto you more than unto God, judge ye.

When the laws of the land conflict with the commands of God, then a Christian is right to obey God rather than man.

Q. First Corinthians 6:1–11 warns Christians not to go to court against each other. Is there ever a time when a Christian can sue another Christian?

A. Verse one says, "Dare any of you, having a matter against another, go to law before the unjust, and not before the saints?" He does not say that Christians are not to go to law. If Christians did not use the benefit of the law, they would suffer great loss at the hands of the unsaved. He is saying that Christians should not go to law against each other—Christian against Christian. The differences between believers are not to be taken to a secular court; they should be settled by believers. This is something which churches and believers in general ignore today.

After I had come to Southern California as a pastor I was rather amazed one day when a man came in and wanted to bring a charge against an officer of the church. He claimed this man had cheated him in a business deal. He said, "Now I want you to bring him up before the board and make him settle with me." I told him, "I think you are approaching this the right way. When can you appear before the board and make your charges?" "Oh," he said, "I've told you about it. That is all that is necessary." I pointed out to him that I had no way to verify the charge; both men would need to appear before the board. Then I asked him, "Would you be willing to accept the verdict of the board?" "Well," he said, "it all depends on how they decided it. If they decided in my favor, I would accept it." So then I asked him if he would accept the verdict if it were against him, and he assured me that he would not. Of course, I told him that we might as well forget the whole matter. I said, "You are not really willing to turn this issue over to the other believers for a verdict."

Church fights should not be aired in state courts before unbelievers. Individual differences among Christians should be adjudicated by believers. It is bad enough when two Christians are divorced, but it is an extremely serious matter when Christians go before a secular court and air their differences before unbelievers. When a Christian couple comes to me and tells me they simply cannot get along, and I see there is no way of working out a reconciliation, I advise a legal separation, not a court trial.

Why should a believer let other believers be the judges rather than take his case to the unsaved world for their judgment? Again, this does not forbid a Christian from going to court with an unbeliever, but why should two believers bring their differences to be settled by other believers? Paul gives three reasons in 1 Corinthians 6 regarding the capabilities of believers to judge.

- Saints will judge the world. *"Do ye not know that the saints shall judge the world? and if the world shall be judged by you, are ye unworthy to judge the smallest matters?"* (v. 2).

- Saints will judge angels. *"Know ye not that we shall judge angels? how much more things that pertain to this life?"* (v. 3).

- Unrighteousness is not in the kingdom. *"Know ye not that the unrighteous shall not inherit the kingdom of God? Be not deceived: neither fornicators, nor idolaters, nor adulterers, nor effeminate, nor abusers of themselves with mankind, nor thieves, nor covetous, nor drunkards, nor revilers, nor extortioners, shall inherit the kingdom of God"* (vv. 9–10).

No secular judge or jury is equipped to make spiritual decisions because they do not comprehend spiritual principles. That is why court cases that pertain to churches and Christians go haywire the minute they hit the legal mills. A secular judge may know the material in the law books, but he knows nothing about spiritual decisions. He has no spiritual discernment.

Following a trial here in Southern California I looked at the jury shown on television and said to my wife, "I thank God my life is not in the hands of the twelve people I see there." After the trial was over some of the jurors made statements for the television program which revealed that they were not capable of judging the case. Yet Christians will trust that crowd rather than take their cases to other believers who do have spiritual discernment. "I speak to your shame. Is it so, that there is not a wise man among you? no, not one that shall be able to judge between his brethren? But brother goeth to law with brother, and that before the unbelievers" (vv. 5–6). Of course not every Christian is a capable judge, but Paul is saying, "I speak to your shame; isn't there a wise man among you?" When you go to a secular court, you are saying that *none* of the saints are capable of judging. Well, I know some dear brethren in the Lord with whom I would be willing to risk my life. I am confident they would render a just verdict.

HANDICAPPED

Q. Does God make people crippled, blind, or deaf to use them or their circumstances to bring them to Christ? I've heard Exodus 4:11 and Isaiah 45:7 quoted to support the idea that He does.

A. May I say, that's an entirely wrong way to express it. The quotation that is given in Exodus 4:11 says, "And the LORD said unto him [Moses], Who hath made man's mouth? or who maketh the dumb, or deaf, or the seeing, or the blind? have not I, the LORD?" The whole point of that passage of Scripture is not that God made them disabled, but that God made the mouth and the other parts of our bodies. They become distorted because of sin. It is the presence of sin that has brought sorrow and death to the human family. Our sins are what bring tragedy into our lives. God set that up at the very beginning, and anything that is contrary to Him must always result in tragedy and sorrow. It can't be otherwise.

Now I'm going over to Isaiah 45:7: "I form the light, and create darkness: I make peace, and create evil: I the LORD do all these things." The word that is translated *evil* here is the Hebrew word *ra*, which could have been translated sorrow, wretchedness, adversity, afflictions, or calamities. But it is never translated *sin*. In other words, God created evil only in the sense that He made sorrow and wretchedness and all of these things to be the fruit and the result of sin.

This is not to say that personal sin is the only reason for suffering or disability. There are other reasons, such as a stand for righteousness, a high purpose of God, or our heavenly Father's discipline. But this introduces an entirely different subject.

HOMOSEXUALITY

Q. What do you think about women who dress like men and partake of men's sports activities, preferring men's company? And what do you think of men who wear women's underthings and paint their faces and nails and wear loud perfumes and even women's dresses?

A. Well, I want to say to you that those who do that sort of thing are highly suspect today and rightly so, because it is one of the marks of some homosexuals. By the way, I believe that in Old Testament days the whole point of the law concerning the wearing of clothing designed for the opposite sex was to keep a woman from looking and acting like a man, or a man from looking and acting like a woman in order to prevent homosexuality and lesbianism.

Q. Is AIDS God's curse on homosexual behavior?

A. It would seem so. God deals with this issue in both the Old and the New Testaments. "Thou shalt not lie with mankind, as with womankind: it is abomination" (Lev. 18:22).

Some years ago, right here in downtown Los Angeles, a church put on a dance for sexual perverts. I am told they had over 700 people at that dance. A hard-boiled newspaper writer went to write it up, but walked out in disgust. Yet a "church" hosted that! My friend, God condemns it! In

---

the Old Testament He condemns it; in the New Testament He condemns it.

> Wherefore God also gave them up to uncleanness through the lusts of their own hearts, to dishonour their own bodies between themselves: who changed the truth of God into a lie, and worshipped and served the creature more than the Creator, who is blessed for ever. Amen. For this cause God gave them up unto vile affections: for even their women did change the natural use into that which is against nature: and likewise also the men, leaving the natural use of the woman, burned in their lust one toward another; men with men working that which is unseemly, and receiving in themselves that recompence of their error which was meet. And even as they did not like to retain God in their knowledge, God gave them over to a reprobate mind, to do those things which are not convenient (Rom. 1:24–28).

This depravity is common today. The United States has become like Sodom and Gomorrah. I love this country, and I weep to see the way it is going. I hate to see these dirty, filthy, immoral people bringing us into judgment. Believe me, the judgment of God is already upon us today. These are passions of dishonor and disgrace and depravity, regardless of today's public opinion. Perversion entered into Greek life and brought Greece down to the dust. Go over there and look at Greece today. The glory has passed away. Why? These were their sins.

We find that we can't have peace abroad and we can't have peace at home. Why not? "There is no peace, saith the LORD, unto the wicked" (Isa. 48:22). Along with homosexuality the sin of beastiality is dealt with in Leviticus 18:23. The unspeakable was practiced in the fertility cults and nature worship. Licentiousness is always connected with idolatry in the most debased fashion. And if you think this is not being practiced today, then you should talk to the police department in a city like Los Angeles. They can tell you. The message is clear: "Defile not ye yourselves in any of these things: for in all these the nations are defiled which I cast out before you: And the land is defiled: therefore I do visit the iniquity thereof upon it, and the land itself vomiteth out her inhabitants" (Lev. 18:24–25).

The nations in Palestine were cast out of that land because they committed these abominable and atrocious sins. A lot of soft-hearted and soft-headed preachers today weep because God put out the Canaanites. Here is the reason God put them out—God couldn't tolerate what was taking place. The land of the Canaanites was eaten up with venereal disease. Why do you suppose God told them not to take even a wedge of gold or to touch a garment in the city of Jericho? They were guilty of the vilest sins imaginable. Don't you think that God put them out for a good reason? After all, if the tenant doesn't pay rent, he can be put out, and God happened to own that land!

My friend, that is the way you and I occupy this earth down here. Our "three score years and ten" is just a lease. The land is God's. It would be well for us to make His business our business, because His business is the one that will prevail.

> Ye shall therefore keep my statutes and my judgments, and shall not commit any of these abominations; neither any of your own nation, nor any stranger that sojourneth among you: (For all these abominations have the men of the land done, which were before you, and the land is defiled;) that the land spue not you out also, when ye defile it, as it spued out the nations that were before you. For whosoever shall commit any of these abominations, even the souls that commit them shall be cut off from among their people. Therefore shall ye keep mine ordinance, that ye commit not any one of these abominable customs, which were committed before you, and that ye defile not your-

selves therein: I am the LORD *your God* (Lev. 18:26–30).

God gives a double warning to His people that if they pursue a pattern similar to the one that preceded them in the land, the same judgment, if not worse, would befall them. God's land must be holy. God's ultimate goal is that righteousness will cover the earth.

Q. I am ashamed to go to our pastor to seek help. My son is a homosexual. I am divorced and remarried to a fine Christian, and we have a good Christian marriage which neither of us had before. You have mentioned that you have received letters from people who were once homosexuals and are no longer. That is what I want for my son. No one in my family has confronted him about it, yet none of the men in the family like him or want to be around him. How can I handle this?

A. Let me say that I was a pastor for forty years, and I found this feeling toward the pastor to be common. I wish people could go to their pastors and just lay it all out before him. I have had problems presented to me since I have been on radio that I never even heard about when I was a pastor.

I have an answer for you and it will be brief, but may I say to you, I think the homosexual today has presented a real problem to the church. I do not think a person living as a homosexual ought to be accepted into the membership of the church. They have to first be converted. Homosexuality is a sin according to the Bible.

Now may I say to you that our attitude toward the homosexual should be the same as our attitude toward any other sinner who needs a Savior. I think the attitude of your family toward this boy is wrong. You will never win him as long as you treat him like he's the off-scouring of the earth, though his lifestyle is a terrible thing. He needs your love right now as he has never needed it before. He needs your

interest, he needs your care, he needs your help. For goodness sake, don't turn your back on your boy at this time
because of this awful thing he is in. He can be delivered.

As you have said, we have literally hundreds of letters
from those who have been delivered from homosexual living. I know they can be converted, but they can never be
converted if you show the attitude that you and your family
are showing toward the boy. Love him, in spite of what he
is, and do everything to try to convert him!

PACIFISM

Q. Scripture says to do all things diligently for the Lord,
so how can I put old things of the flesh behind me—
like immorality, impure passion, evil desire, greed, and
anger—and then go to war and kill someone and say I did it
in the name of Christ and His love? Or if someone wants to
take advantage of me and persecute me unjustly by stealing
my possessions, and Jesus says give them my shirt also,
how could I kill someone for something that isn't supposed
to matter that much to me?

A. Well, I think you have built up a philosophy of life
that is entirely foreign to the Scripture, and yet you
have pulled out of Scripture certain verses. You have forgot-
ten that you are not only a citizen of heaven, but you are a
citizen of a country down here.

Let's go back to the very beginning. The Scripture
says, "Thou shalt not kill." So many use that as their reason
for not going to war. They also apply it to capital punishment. They say, "Thou shalt not kill," but that very commandment is based on what God said to Noah, "Whoso
sheddeth man's blood, by man shall his blood be shed"
(Gen. 9:6). So God has given an authority to human government.

The Scriptures (and you need to put a few other Scriptures with the ones that you are using) deal with your responsibility as an individual. Christian responsibility is

one thing, but your responsibility as a citizen of a nation is something also that needs to be recognized. You ask, is that scriptural? In Romans 13 Paul writes about Christian conduct:

> Let every soul be subject unto the higher powers. For there is no power but of God: the powers that be are ordained of God. Whosoever therefore resisteth the power, resisteth the ordinance of God: and they that resist shall receive to themselves damnation [that is, judgment]. For rulers are not a terror to good works, but to the evil. Wilt thou then not be afraid of the power? do that which is good, and thou shalt have praise of the same (vv. 1–3).

Now may I say to you that you and I have a responsibility to our government, and we have to pay taxes. I don't like to pay taxes, and I am opposed to the tremendous taxes that we are having to pay today. And I want the government to quit putting up all these great buildings and having all of these different departments functioning that are absolutely nonessential, certainly for taxpayers who are overburdened today. Nevertheless, we have to pay taxes, even to a corrupt government.

Unfortunately, I'm afraid the past few wars we have fought were not for any great cause. Yet World War I was fought "to make the world safe for democracy." What a joke that turned out to be! And we were going to "deliver the world from Nazism" in World War II, but what did we do? We delivered the world over to communism. It was like Tweedle Dum and Tweedle Dee—one is just as bad as the other. May I say to you, I feel that at the top our government hasn't had the best leadership it should have had. Yet you and I have a responsibility as citizens to our government.

Today if a war should break out and we were attacked, I am confident that, with the feeling as it is, many would not take up arms. But I do believe that every Christian would have a responsibility to defend his country. I believe that is scriptural.

So your argument is actually not valid at all, because being passive as a Christian in your own personal life is one thing. But when your government, your country, is attacked, you need to defend it. You are acting as a minister of God to execute justice in the earth.

SELF-DEFENSE

Q. Should a Christian defend himself against an intruder? I believe that God would not expect us to remain idle, but others in my Bible class believe we shouldn't resist because, they say, there is no Bible reference to the contrary.

A. First of all, today there is a namby-pamby way of thinking that a Christian is not to defend himself. Scripture tells us we are to resist evil (see James 4:7; 1 Peter 5:9). I would say that if a man entered your house with a gun, to resist him would be to resist evil. The Lord Jesus said, "A strong man armed keepeth his house." Now what is the purpose of his being armed? Well, the Lord Jesus said the strong man will keep his house and will protect it.

Now let me try to show how utterly preposterous and ridiculous the idea is that we are not to defend ourselves. Suppose you are a husband and at home when a man breaks into your house. He is going to rape your wife and kill your daughter. Are you to just sit there and take it? I don't think so. I don't think the Scripture teaches anything like that at all; the Scripture verses that are being used have been taken out of context.

True, in the Sermon on the Mount it says "resist not evil." What does that mean? Well, to begin with, the Sermon on the Mount is the law of the kingdom. When Christ reigns you will be able to take the locks off your doors because, after all, a lock on the door is there to resist evil. I think that we *are* to resist evil today, and I'd advise you to keep those locks on there. I see no reason why Christians should not defend themselves the best they possibly can. To take a position that we are not to resist today is very foolish and in my opinion unscriptural.

Q. You embarrassed me when you advocated firearms in the household based on an Old Testament admonition concerning the house as a stronghold. You seem to forget that you live in a "shoot first and ask questions later" society, quite the antithesis of what Christ was all about.

A. To begin with, I do not base this on the Old Testament; the Lord Jesus said that a strong man armed keeps his household: "When a strong man armed keepeth his palace, his goods are in peace" (Luke 11:21). That is, to protect his home if he didn't have a sword he'd get one. And today he'd get a pistol, I think.

Now I recognize that I am touching a very sore spot, so consider the problem about getting rid of the guns. When you say that the gun shoots people, I think you are wrong. A gun never shoots; it is the person who handles the gun who shoots. The problem is not with the gun, the problem is with the individual.

A gun is a protection for the home. Because a gun may go off accidentally, it should be handled very carefully and not be put where children can get it. It is tragic when a young person kills his friend or his brother because he picked up a gun. He didn't mean to shoot anyone, but he did. I think all too often parents are not using proper care in teaching the use of a gun. I remember when I was a boy my dad took me out hunting and spent an entire afternoon explaining how to load and carry a gun and how, when you go through a fence, to always keep the barrel pointed down. It's best to lean the gun against a post. Never swing it around. It could shoot in any direction. And if other people are around, you are to exercise judgment in the use of a gun.

The fact of the matter is, there are more people here in California being killed by automobiles than are being killed by guns. If you got rid of the automobile, you would eliminate a lot of people being killed.

You see, we are handling the problem from the wrong end. No Christian is going to shoot at anyone without provocation. Now the Lord Jesus is the One who said, "A strong man armed keepeth his palace." As I see it, that means you ought to have a gun to protect your loved ones.

I knew a man who thought that as a Christian he ought not have a gun. Two men broke in one night with guns. By the way, a thief always will be able to get one. They broke in and stole everything he had. They got quite a bit of money and jewelry and they raped his wife. And he said, "If I had had a gun I could have protected my loved one and my property. I wish I'd had a gun."

Frankly, friend, I wish he had had one, too. A Christian can certainly use a gun for self-protection. I consider that to be very scriptural.

You and I live in a big, bad world. The problem is that the crazy maniacs should be locked up and those who commit crimes should be punished, but we have a lot of softhearted judges who do not enforce the law. And until the law is enforced, you are going to have to protect yourself. I personally think it is going to get worse.

I recognize that what I am saying is not popular right now. The lovey-dovey stuff is popular. Unless you have been a victim, you are not going to agree with me. But if you have been a victim, you are going to agree with everything I say.

So I would advise you to protect yourself. Please don't go around shooting people indiscriminately, but if somebody comes around to shoot you and your loved ones, you ought to be able to protect yourself and them.

Q. You expressed great sympathy and compassion for the victims of violent crime, which I share. But the Christian is to exercise sympathy and compassion for the criminal also. God loves not only good men but also bad men.

A. First, may I say that somebody ought to express sympathy for the victims because there is very little expressed for them today. You can shoot down a policeman in Southern California, and it is just a ho-hum announcement on the news media. You don't see anybody marching or anybody taking exception to it at all. He was shot in the line of duty, and that's that. But let the policeman shoot somebody and, my gracious alive, you have a furor over that!

My question then to you would be, does the sympathy and compassion a Christian has for a murderer mean we should turn him loose? I don't think so. These bleeding hearts are the ones who protest and march and give the impression that we don't want the murderers punished. You can't walk on the streets in my city at night—and some places you dare not walk in the daytime—because the criminal is not being punished. Christian compassion does not mean you are not to punish the murderer.

You say that God loves not only good men but bad men. And I say you are wrong. God does not love good men. God loves bad men. The Scripture says repeatedly that there is not one good; no, not one. Jesus said there is none good but God (see Luke 18:19). So there are not any good men for God to love. He loves only bad men. That is the whole point, and I'm afraid you've missed it.

We make a great deal of the fact that the Lord Jesus said, "Father, forgive them, for they know not what they do." Those men who crucified our Lord didn't know they were crucifying the Son of God. The centurion did know before it was over, but by then he had already put Jesus on the cross and watched Him die. The supernatural darkness had already come, during which time the Lord Jesus had dismissed His spirit. He was dead on the cross. Those who crucified Him were actually committing the worst possible sin by crucifying the Son of God. But Jesus had said, "Father, forgive them." They were not lost because of crucifying Him. That is the whole point. They were lost because they were sinners. We are told that some who were responsible for Christ's crucifixion, including some of the priests, subsequently did believe on Him, and they were saved. But that hasn't anything in the world to do with the punishing of criminals.

I think you are becoming a "bleeding heart" when, in your letter, you use Christ's words on the cross, "Father, forgive them," as the reason we should let criminals off today.

God makes it very clear He is going to judge, and He makes no apology for that judgment. At the end there will be a great company of people who are going to endure the second death, and He is going to be the executioner. He is not only the Savior, He is also the Judge. We need to have a right perspective and a well-balanced view of our wonderful Lord Jesus.

TOBACCO

Q. According to the Scriptures, is it a sin to use tobacco?

A. Well, to begin with, tobacco is never even mentioned in the Word of God. And I do not think tobacco ought to be put on the same moral level as liquor. Years ago, a dear old grandmother who smoked a pipe helped me a great deal. Tobacco is in a little different classification, the way I understand it. However, a person is a fool to smoke cigarettes considering the danger of cancer of the lungs. I know what that is. I've had cancer of the lungs, but it wasn't caused by cigarettes because I never smoked cigarettes. And may I say to you again, knowing how terrible an operation on the lungs is, you are a fool to smoke a cigarette.